EVERYTHING

YOU NEED TO KNOW ABOUT...

Horses

EVERYTHING
YOU NEED TO KNOW ABOUT...
Horses

CHERYL KIMBALL

David & Charles

A DAVID & CHARLES BOOK

David & Charles is a subsidiary of F+W (UK) Ltd.,

an F+W Publications Inc. company

First published in the UK in 2004

First published in the USA as The Everything® Horse Book,

by Adams Media Corporation in 2002

Project Manager Ian Kearey

Cover Design Ali Myer

A catalogue record for this book is available from the British Library.

ISBN 0 7153 2060 2

Printed in Great Britain by CPI Bath

for David & Charles

Brunel House   Newton Abbot   Devon

Visit our website at www.davidandcharles.co.uk

David & Charles books are available from all good bookshops;

alternatively you can contact our Orderline on (0)1626 334555 or

write to us at FREEPOST EX2110, David & Charles Direct,

Newton Abbot, TQ12 4ZZ (no stamp required UK mainland).

DEDICATION

To Pat and Breezy, Karen and Alana, who started it all;

to everyone involved with Piper Ridge Farm in Limerick, Maine,
USA, including a world-class line-up of trainers, who keep me
on track as best they can, given my ability;

to my parents, who, although they may not have given in
to my pleas for a horse, definitely taught me to love
and respect animals;

to Jack, who seems to think it is natural that I consider the
animals under my care to be my friends;

and, although it is part of their charm that they will never
read this book, to my horse friends, past, present and future.
If this book helps even one human to treat even one horse with
the respect and care horses deserve, it will have been worth all
the hours it took to write it.

Contents

Acknowledgments

Thanks to: Sue Ducharme, riding pal, expert wordsmith and crafter of
Chapter 10; Lesley Bolton, who as I write this section is in the process of
making the rest of the book into something better than it was when
she received it; and anyone else I pestered with questions – whether or not
they knew I was writing a book. These people and many others helped
make this book the best it could be; any factual errors in this book are
all mine and will gratefully be corrected if brought to my attention.

Introduction

When I was a child, I was drawn to horses like a magnet to metal. When Helene – the only girl in my neighbourhood to own a horse – and her chestnut gelding, Rowdy, raced past our house, I didn't hide my envy. My friends and I 'played horses' in the primary school playground; the fire escape supports, where we returned to rest and nicker at each other after a good gallop around the school building, served as stables. My family always indulged my obsession with gifts of horse statues, horse pins, horse books – and occasionally the dreaded horse needlepoint pillow – but, alas, never an actual horse.

It wasn't until I was in my late teens that real horses became a big part of my life. My friend Karen and I would hop into my car on beautiful sunny days, wind open the sun roof and race off to our friend Pat's to ride her horses. We were lucky to live near the coast and woods, and we could ride for miles across sandy beaches and along forest paths; indoor arenas were simply not a part of our horse world back then.

When I left school, Karen prophesied, 'I know you'll have a horse of your own some day.' Finally, at the age of 20, I did get a horse, a young mare. But after two years of fun as well as frustration, a job and a boyfriend began to take up what time I had. Horses were relegated to a less important position; I sold my little mare and didn't really think much about horses for over a decade.

At about 34, I had become settled in a career and a long-term relationship. I took a couple of riding lessons late one winter, just for fun. Then, on a whim, I went to visit my horse friend Pat, whom I hadn't seen in years, and horses suddenly became of interest to me again. She had a young gelding for sale – 'Cheap', she announced, the minute I walked through the door. I bought him, and the rest, as they say, is history.

Through a series of events instigated by the fact that I had this two-year-old horse to work with and no idea how to do it, I became involved in a philosophy of horsemanship sometimes referred to as 'natural horsemanship' (discussed in Chapter 12) that fulfils me both intellectually and physically; I think about horses all the time, and I haven't seen the inside of a fitness centre since I bought that young gelding. I have come to thoroughly enjoy working with young horses, and cannot imagine ever again being without the company of a horse.

The key to having fun with horses, I think, is to remember that they are horses. They are not puppies, and cannot be treated like puppies without seriously endangering your life. They are not children, despite various attempts to approach them with psychological profiles more suited to children. That said, I'm not suggesting that you don't pamper your horses – give them treats (in their buckets, though, not out of your hand – see Chapter 11 for my opinion on that), coo at them, go crazy and put holiday decorations on their stable doors (out of reach of the horse, please!) – but never underestimate their strength and their self-preservation instinct. Grant them their horse qualities.

Respect your horses as living, breathing, decision-making animals, and treat them in a manner that will encourage their respect for you (rather than their fear of you!) in return. From this approach, you will have a partnership beyond imagination with a half-ton animal that could crush you like a fly, but wouldn't even dream of it because you have proven that you are 100 per cent reliable in a world full of horse-eating monsters. When your horse prefers to be with you more than anything else on the planet, it is both an honour and a privilege beyond your wildest dreams. When I go to the pasture and my mare leaves her horse friends to come and see me, get a little scratch and blow her silky breath on my neck, someone could be knocking at the door with a million-pound cheque for me, and I wouldn't move to get it.

I hope this book serves as enough of an introduction to horses for you to also take one more step along the path to being unfulfilled without the company of horses. There's an endless amount to be learned – both through books and mostly from the horses themselves – and I can practically guarantee that you will never be bored again with a horse or two in your life.

I wish you the best in all your equine endeavours. Above all, stay safe, and may your paths and those of your equine companions be lined with good footing and topped by cloudless blue skies.

CHAPTER 1

History of the Horse

The evolution of the horse is a well-studied topic; in fact, archaeologists have discovered the fossils of a complete horse skeleton. Nonetheless, research shows some contradictions in the details of when and where horses were domesticated and ridden. New information continues to unfold. And who knows – another significant discovery could be made any minute. One thing is certain, though: humans and horses have an interrelated history.

This chapter offers a chronological look at some of the highlights of the current facts known about the early evolution of the horse. It also includes information about periods in which the use of the horse was significant, such as in times of war.

The Ancient Horse

75 Million Years Ago

The earliest ancestor to all hoofed animals is *Condylarthra*, which lived over 75 million years ago. *Condylarthra* had five toes on each limb, was the size of a fox, and was a herbivore that lived in the swamplands of the Northern Hemisphere.

What is a herbivore?
A **herbivore** is an animal that subsists totally on plant life. Horses are herbivores. This distinction makes the horse a prey animal (with those that hunt them considered predators), a fact that contributes greatly to the overall behaviour of the species.

55 Million Years Ago

Hyracotherium was a family of leaf browsers that was descended from *Condylarthra*. Most *Hyracotherium* had four toes on each limb, with the exception of one variety, which had only three working toes on its hind feet. This unique variety is the first 'horse', which appeared on Earth approximately 55 million years ago, at the beginning of the Eocene Epoch. Fossils of *Eohippus*, as these first horses have been named by archaeologists, showed the mammal to be smaller than a medium-sized dog. *Eohippus* lived primarily in North America.

25 Million Years Ago

As the Eocene Epoch gave way to the Miocene Epoch around 25 million years ago, *Eohippus* evolved into the three-toed *Mesohippus*, then into *Mercyhippus*; this still had three toes, but one of them was more prominent. The toe of the horse wasn't the only thing to evolve. The tooth structure began to develop to accommodate the changing food source as the Miocene Epoch brought open grasslands. In turn, the skull became larger to accommodate larger teeth. As the skull became larger, the rest of the animal adapted to support the changing weight distribution.

Part of the way up the horse's leg, past the knee on the inside, is what seems to be a calloused piece of skin usually around the size of two 20p pieces. Called the chestnut, this is said to be what remains of the first of the three toes that the horse lost during its evolution. The two other toe vestiges can be found as a hard nodule behind the fetlock – the ergot.

6 Million Years Ago

Changing habitat from swamplands to dry savannahs caused the horse to evolve from a creature with multiple toes to one with a single toe, which is better adapted to roaming across dry ground. We can thank the Pliocene Epoch for *Pliohippus*, the first single-toed horse, which served as a prototype for our own *Equus*. *Pliohippus* had a ligament-sprung hoof and longer legs with flexing ligaments, which gave way to a running action similar to that of the modern horse.

1 Million Years Ago

The evolution from *Pliohippus* to *Equus* took place over five million years. Due to changes in climate and land mass during this time, *Equus* found its way from North America to South America and spread across Asia, Europe and Africa.

The following table summarizes the evolution of the horse.

	EVOLUTION OF THE HORSE	
Eohippus	Four toes	55 million years ago
Mesohippus	Three toes	25 million years ago
Mercyhippus	Three toes	20 million years ago
Pliohippus	One toe	6 million years ago
Equus	One toe	1 million years ago

30,000 Years Ago

An ivory horse carved from a mammoth tusk, which was found in a cave in Germany, has been dated at around 30,000 years old. The very worn carving, measuring 6.3cm (2¹/₂in) long, is believed to have been carried for good luck during hunts for horse meat.

12,000 Years Ago

A cave drawing from this period has been found in Puerte Viesgo in Spain. The drawing shows a horse wearing what appears to be a primitive sort of bridle, but no other significant evidence has been found to verify humans riding horses in this early age – the same period as the domestication of the dog – although some scant evidence has emerged that horses were in fact ridden as much as 3,000 years earlier than this.

According to Xenophon (430–355BCE): 'If one induces the horse to assume that carriage which it would adopt of its own accord when displaying its beauty, then one directs the horse to appear joyous and magnificent, proud and remarkable for having been ridden.'

8,000 Years Ago

The equid disappeared from the North American continent during this period, and to this day, no definitive explanation for this disappearance has been determined. Horses did not return to North America until the 15th century CE.

4000–3000BCE

This is considered to be the true age of the domestication of the horse. Up to this point, horses were merely a source of food and, therefore, an object of prey. The domestication of the horse has been thought to have first taken place on the steppes north of the Black Sea. Evidence found in China of mounted warriors supports the theory that horses were extensively ridden for the first time around 4000BCE.

SIX EQUIDS IN EXISTENCE TODAY	
Equus burchelli	The plains zebra of Africa
Equus zebra	The mountain zebra of South Africa
Equus grevyi	The most horse-like zebra
Equus caballus	The domestic horse
Equus hemonius	The ass of Asia and the Middle East
Equus asinus	The ass and the donkey of northern Africa

2000BCE

The horse was thought to have been first harnessed in the Near East around this time. Evidence of man's early interactions with the horse comes mostly in the form of tapestries, relief pottery and other works of art, depicting battle scenes and exemplifying the human reverence for the horse's beauty.

In 1994, Dr David Anthony and Dorcas Brown founded the Institute for Ancient Equestrian Studies in the Department of Anthropology at Hartwick College in Oneonta, New York, USA. The institute, which is dedicated to archaeological research concerning the origins of horse riding and the impact of riding on human society, is affiliated with the Institute for the History and Archaeology of the Volga in Samara, Russia.

1500BCE

Horses began to be used more widely in agricultural work. Initially, they were hitched up with oxen yokes, but the design cut off the horse's wind, so a padded collar was designed to better suit the horse. Metal snaffle bits were perfected to take the place of nose rings, which had been used to control the animal. In China, horses were used to pull chariots.

1350BCE

The first records of systematic training, conditioning and taking care of horses date from this time. They were written by a man named Kikkuli, who was a Mittani, an Aryan group that had cultural ties to India. Tablets have been found that showed Kikkuli's instructions to the Hittite rulers prescribing the care of harness racing horses. The Hittites, although clearly gaining their equestrian knowledge from other peoples, were credited with the development of the Arab horse and were noted for their highly mobile equestrian troops.

500BCE

Well into the last centuries BCE, horse riding had not only been mastered but was also common. Scythian warriors, who had the first recorded geldings and whose wealth was measured in horses, were skilled in the art of battle on horseback. Since they believed that their wealth followed them to the afterworld, many artefacts have been found in their burial grounds – sometimes hundreds of horses were buried with them.

Significant Recent Equine Discoveries

1879

Marcelino de Sautuola, a Spanish engineer who was also a serious amateur archaeologist, was exploring a cave with his five-year-old daughter in the mountains of southern France when she noticed on the cave ceiling drawings that included horses. Studies of these drawings in the now-famous Altamira cave have determined that they are from a period between 30,000 and 10,000 years ago.

1881

In 1881, a wild herd of *Equus przewalskii*, considered to be the forebear of all domestic horses, was discovered in Mongolia.

1920

Parts of a horse skull were discovered in Kent by Sir Richard Owen. Originally classified as *Hyracotherium*, after further discoveries around the world, the skull was eventually reclassified as *Eohippus*.

Przewalskii's horse was discovered in the remote regions of Mongolia in 1881 by the Russian explorer Nikolai Mikhailovich Przewalskii. It is believed to be the closest ancestor to the ancient horse in existence. Described as being around 12 hands with a stocky body and short legs, it currently is believed to be extinct in the wild, although attempts are now being made to reintroduce it.

1940

Four teenagers discovered the Lascaux Caves in southern France. The walls of different rooms in the cave are heavily illustrated, including drawings of many horses that resemble the present-day Przewalskii's horse. According to research, the paintings date back 17,000 years, to the Magdalenian Age. Many websites offer views of the cave, which has been closed to the public since 1963. Check out the official website at *www.culture.fr/culture/arcnat/lascaux/en/*.

1950

In 1950, scientists began using carbon isotopes (carbon dating) to determine the age of ancient objects. This allowed for much more accurate classification and identification of archaeological findings.

Horses in North America

The Great Disappearing Act

One of the great mysteries of the horse is its disappearance 8,000 years ago from the North American continent, despite the fact that *Eohippus* evolved there over a period of millions of years. The horse migrated south to South America and west across the land bridge of what is now the Bering Strait into Asia. Further climate and geographical changes during the Ice Age pushed horses further into the Middle East and Africa. It is believed that those that remained in North America succumbed to a fatal disease.

Many Thanks, Spanish Conquistadors!

The horse was being ridden and domesticated and becoming a crucial member of civilization in other parts of the world long before it reappeared in North America. In fact, it didn't reappear until the 15th century. Christopher Columbus is credited with this reappearance: he took horses to the West Indies. Ponce de Leon is thought to be responsible for introducing Andalucian-bred stock into what is now Florida.

By the 17th century, Native American tribes along the Mexican border had begun to use horses, as had American settlers in the West. In addition, the Native Americans used horses to barter with other tribes, which allowed the horse to move across the rest of the western United States. Some of these horses escaped captivity, thus marking the beginning of the wild (or, more accurately, feral) horse bands in the American West.

Horses in Modern Battle

Ancient civilizations utilized the horse in battle to carry soldiers and pull chariots, making armies mobile in some of the harshest climates in the world. The horse has been heavily used in modern warfare as well:

- The Boer War in South Africa (1899–1902) produced a huge demand for horses, mules and donkeys. Thousands of wild horses in America were captured and shipped overseas; over 500,000 were said to have died during the course of the war.
- Horses were also in great demand during World War I. Records show that hundreds of thousands were abandoned in the deserts.
- In 1939, the Polish army is noted to have had 86,000 horses; the Germans, almost 1,200,000.

Solving Mysteries of the Past

Many books have been written about the evolution of the horse. Although you will find differing opinions and even small contradictions in factual details from one book to the next, what is consistent throughout is a well-deserved reverence and fascination by humans for an animal that has made an undeniable contribution to the advancement and civilization of humankind.

Discoveries are still being made about the horse, and even small finds can change some major assumptions. For instance, it was long thought that early domestication of the horse did not include any significant riding by humans. However, later excavations of horse skulls with teeth worn presumably by bits show that riding actually occurred much earlier than archaeologists had first believed – in fact, 3,000 years earlier. It's hard to keep up with the horse!

CHAPTER 2

Horse Breeds

All horses are fundamentally the same – they exhibit basically the same herd behaviour, possess a strong sense of self-preservation, and have four legs and a tail. However, there are dozens of breeds, and each one has different physical and, to some degree, behavioural characteristics.

Horse lovers typically favour a particular breed or two, usually due to the breed's physical appearance or the kind of horse-related activity or sport the person wants to undertake. This chapter takes a look at the differences and similarities among breeds.

Finding Your Favourite Breed

Plenty of good riding horses are not any particular breed – they might be a cross between two or more different breeds, such as a Welsh Cob and an Arab, or an Irish Draught and a Thoroughbred. In 'For sale' adverts descriptions such as 'Three-quarter Thoroughbred mare' or 'Welsh cross Arab gelding' show that a horse is not purebred. However, we all have our favourite breeds, and when we are looking for a horse to buy, we will take its parentage into account.

I have two Quarter Horses, and while there is something about the physical sturdiness of this breed that I like a lot, I find myself also attracted to the Arab breed, and have finally bought a yearling Arab to add to my growing collection. Despite the opinions of a few people I spoke to when I was looking for an Arab to purchase, I have found that I can handle and educate my Arab in the same way that I did my Quarter Horse youngsters, and with the same level of success. However, even with all the similarities among my horses, there are differences. For one thing, my Arab has taken a lot longer to develop physically than the Quarter Horses did. I didn't start her under saddle until she was three, whereas my Quarter Horses were well-developed enough to start under saddle and ride (at least lightly) as two- and three-year-olds. As for behaviour, my Arab's personality is very different from that of my two Quarter Horses, but each of the latter are significantly different from each other as well. So I remain convinced that Arabs can be handled in the same manner as Quarter Horses.

If you find a breed that you like, talk to a breeder about why he or she picked it to concentrate in. What does the breeder do with his or her horses? What do the people who buy this breed tend to do with them? Watch the horses interact with each other; watch them being ridden, driven or handled. Handle and ride one yourself if possible – hands-on research is always the best way to find out.

Maybe you'll ultimately decide that a horse is a horse is a horse, and that breed matters little when the time comes to buy one of your own. But you have to narrow your search down somehow, and breed is certainly a reasonable place to start.

Common Riding Horses

There are some breeds of horses that are more common than others, mainly because they make good riding horses or have some physical asset that makes them attractive. Thoroughbreds are popular because of their racing ability, while Arabs are loved for their looks as well as their fantastic endurance over long distances.

What is a hand?
In horsey terms, a **hand** is the unit used to measure horse height. One hand equals 10cm (4in), so a horse that stands 15 hands tall is 1.52m (5ft) tall at the wither.

Thoroughbred

This is the breed that the non-horse world is most familiar with because of its predominance on the racecourse. The Thoroughbred horse tends to stand in excess of 16 hands, and its ancestry, along with that of many other breeds, can be traced back to the Arab horse. The Thoroughbred's tall, lean conformation makes it a perfect candidate for racing. In fact, this breed is capable of a single stride of over 6m (20ft) and of speeds of up to 64kmph (40mph). The Thoroughbred has come to be considered a great horse to mix with the pedigrees of other breeds.

Characteristics of the Thoroughbred include a tall, slender frame, good for racing like the wind for long distances; a great lung capacity; and a strong competitive spirit. Thoroughbreds start their race training very young, typically working mounted in their yearling year and going on to professional racing as two-year-olds.

Many Thoroughbreds are retired from racing by the time they are five years old – an age when most other horses are just starting their riding careers in earnest! The best of the best of these retired Thoroughbreds are used for breeding, and the rest are often sold at reasonable prices to equestrians looking for dressage, three-day event or jumping prospects.

You need to be very careful and very knowledgeable when purchasing a retired racehorse. Although lameness is perhaps the most commonly pervasive issue, this usually does not significantly affect the Thoroughbred's performance as a pleasure mount.

Arab

The Arab is perhaps the breed most often visualized when horses are imagined. Characterized by a 'dished' face, flowing mane and high-held tail, the Arab originated in the desert regions of Arabia, and it is this that has given it its ability to cover long distances at speed. Arabs and Arab crosses are renowned for excelling at endurance.

Arabs are truly unique in that their spines have one fewer vertebra than other horses. This means that they can be more difficult to fit with a saddle, because their backs are comparatively short. They are known to be slow to mature, and are said to not be fully grown until they are around seven or eight years old.

Believed to be the oldest pure breed in existence, the Arab has such strong and distinctive characteristics that it has often been used to increase the quality of other breeds. For example, Arab stallions were used in the creation of the Thoroughbred, and many years ago they were also used on Dartmoor and in the New Forest to improve the local ponies.

One of the most attractive aspects of the Arab is its action, which, at its best, makes the horse look as if it is floating along just above the ground; this is particularly noticeable at the trot. Arabs have a reputation for being 'fizzy'. This is mainly because they are very sensitive and react quickly to anything happening in their surroundings, but with careful training they can be wonderful and affectionate riding horses. There are a few different types of Arab, including:

- The Egyptian type, which tends towards a slender frame with a clearly dished face.
- The Polish type, which is stockier in build.

Warmbloods

Warmbloods are extremely popular riding and competition horses. There are several different types: Dutch Warmblood, Danish Warmblood,

Hanoverian (from Germany), Selle Français (from France) and Trakehner (from Poland). All have been developed by breeders looking for the perfect competition horse; something that can jump like a stag and yet has the elegance necessary to perform well at dressage.

Most warmbloods have been produced by crossing local draught breeds (cold-bloods) with Thoroughbreds (hot-bloods). For example, the Dutch Warmblood was created from the Gelderlander and the Groningen, both carriage horses, with the addition of some Thoroughbred to get rid of the more unattractive characteristics associated with driving horses, such as straight shoulders and a high head carriage.

Mountain and Moorland Breeds

Britain is famous for its wide variety of mountain and moorland breeds, including the Shetland, the Exmoor, the Welsh breeds, the Dartmoor, the Fell, the Dales and the Highland. These ponies share some characteristics:

- They all make extremely good riding ponies.
- They are remarkably sure-footed and have a good weight-carrying ability as well.
- They are all less than 14.2 hands, except for the Welsh Cob, which can be up to 15.2 hands high.

Because they originated in the wild uplands of Britain, they are very hardy and generally healthy, and can survive in difficult conditions. All have a varied diet and most are capable of eating gorse, particularly enjoying the flowers, and holly leaves when the need arises. Being well adapted to survival in places where there is little in the way of grass, these breeds will suffer from weight problems if their grazing is not restricted when they are kept in the rich grassy fields that are typical of lowland Britain.

Exmoor, Dartmoor and New Forest Pony

Exmoors are nearly always brown or bay, with dun-coloured markings on the face and belly and black legs. For extra protection against the weather, their eyes are hooded and they have thick hair growth at the top of their tails. Dartmoors, which were once used as pit ponies in the mining industry, make very good children's ponies, and their conformation makes them very comfortable – not at all ponyish – to ride. Despite always being less than 14 hands high, both the Dartmoor and the Exmoor are capable of carrying an adult with very little trouble.

New Forest Ponies are similar to Dartmoor and Exmoors in that they are small – up to 14.2 hands – and tough, and have evolved to survive heathland conditions. However, the New Forest is close to many of the old trade routes around the south-east of England, which means that the breed has had plenty of different blood put into it over the years. New Forest Ponies are good for riding and less pony-like in their character than many of the native breeds.

Welsh Ponies and the Welsh Cob

The Welsh breeds are divided up into four distinct types: Welsh Mountain Pony (section A); Welsh Pony (section B); Welsh Pony of Cob type (section C); and Welsh Cob (section D). The Welsh Mountain Pony is the smallest, at less than 12 hands high.

All the Welsh breeds are beautiful and tend to be highly intelligent. The Welsh Cob has a distinctive trot; it lifts its front feet very high and from the shoulders, and extends the leg outwards before putting the foot down again. It is a wonderful harness horse and was once commonly used by dairies and bakeries for making deliveries.

Dales and Fell

While the Dales and the Fell are often talked about in the same breath, they are two distinct breeds that share some ancestors but have developed separately – very loosely, the Dales in north-eastern England and the Fell in north-western England. Like the Dartmoor, the Dales were used in mining, to transport loads from underground, and the breed is still famous for its strength and weight-carrying ability. The Fell was also a pack pony, but is lighter than the Dales and was commonly ridden, too. Today, both are valued as trekking horses; they are also used for driving.

Shetland and Highland

The Shetland and the Highland are both natives of Scotland. Being only 10 hands high or smaller, the Shetland is a popular breed for children, while the Highland is a good trekking horse and can be up to 14.2 hands. Both were originally used for pack work and are extremely sure-footed over rough ground. Highlands often have a dark dorsal stripe along their spine, as found in donkeys, and some also have faint dark stripes on the backs of their legs.

Connemara

The Connemara is indigenous to Connemara in western Ireland. Like the other mountain and moorland breeds, it is hardy and sure-footed, and it is a marvellous riding pony, excelling at jumping in particular. Although only up to 14.2 hands high, it makes a good cross with a Thoroughbred, as the result is a bigger horse that is ideal for competing.

The Less Common Breeds

There are plenty of other horse and pony breeds that are very popular in their own countries that are becoming more common in Britain. The best-known of these include the Andalucian, the Appaloosa, the Haflinger and the Icelandic Horse.

Horseshoes are considered lucky only if their open ends face up – to have the open end facing down, according to folklore, is thought to make all the luck run out!

Andalucian

This is a Spanish horse that grows up to 15.2 hands. Most Andalucians are grey, with extremely thick but fine wavy manes and tails. They are good at dressage and have a high-stepping trot and comfortable canter. A Lusitano is the Portuguese version of the Andalucian.

Appaloosa

The spotted horse of North America, the Appaloosa descended from Spanish horses and was developed by Native Americans, especially the Nez Perce and the Palouse tribes. White settlers are said to have referred to them as 'Palouse horses', hence the name.

Appaloosas are used in all equine sports, from jumping to roping, racing and trail riding. The Appaloosa Horse Club was formed in 1938 to preserve the breed. In Britain, Appaloosas are becoming more popular, partly because of their many attractive coat colourings and partly because they make extremely good riding horses and have gentle, unflappable temperaments.

Haflinger

These horses are chestnut or palomino with a flaxen mane and tail. They were widely used as pack ponies until the end of World War II, but are now popular for all types of riding.

Icelandic

The product of a cross between Germanic and Celtic horses brought to Iceland by settlers in 874, Icelandic horses are characteristically small, quick, hardy and strong.

They are late to mature and are generally not ridden until they are five years old, but they usually live for a long time. They come in every common coat colour and are best known for their unusual gaits, including the tolt (a four-beat running walk) and the skeid, both of which are described by riders as 'feeling like you are floating over the ground'.

Icelandic horses were used for transporting goods and people across rugged volcanic terrain and mountains, and their sturdy, sure-footed breeding remains in evidence today. Despite their size, their unique bone density is said to enable them to comfortably carry a 113kg (252lb) rider.

Lippizaner

This breed was founded in 1580 in Austria by Archduke Charles II with stallions imported from Spain. Lippizaners are famous for their association with the Spanish Riding School in Vienna. They are grey and between 15 and 16 hands.

Morgan

It is said that a man called Justin Morgan from Vermont in the USA was the original breeder of this compact little horse breed. The sire, which was also called Justin Morgan, was extraordinarily strong and fast and passed on all his characteristics to his offspring. He was such a successful stud horse that he was eventually bought by the US Army and used to breed cavalry horses.

Quarter Horse

The Quarter Horse is probably the most popular horse breed in the United States. There it has developed into two distinct lines:

- A tall, lean horse that has plenty of Thoroughbred blood in it. In the USA, Thoroughbred-type Quarter Horses are used for English riding disciplines such as eventing, dressage and jumping.
- A short stocky horse, usually referred to as the 'foundation type', that is noted for its muscular, powerful hindquarters. It is used for ranch work as well as barrel racing, cutting, reining and other events where sharp turns, quick bursts of speed and the ability to sit back on the haunches are important characteristics.

Quarter Horses are also well-established on the racing circuit in America. Their propensity as sprinters (the quarter in their name allegedly coming from their racing prowess over a quarter of a mile) is widely admired. In Britain, there is growing support for this versatile breed, which has a reputation for being easy-going, clever and good to work with.

Draught Breeds

Although heavy horses are today less often required to do the everyday work for which they were originally developed, they still have a strong following and are very popular when they do displays at county shows, usually dressed in their full harness with manes and tails plaited and coats shining.

Clydesdale

The Clydesdale, which is used as a draught horse worldwide, originated in Clyde Valley, Lanarkshire, in the 18th century. In America, the breed is well-known for hauling wagons for the Budweiser brewery. Visit the Budweiser Clydesdale website at *www.abclydesdales.com*

Percheron

Dapple grey or black, these heavy draught horses are about 16 hands high. The breed originated in the Le Perch region of Normandy in France. Percherons are among the most elegant of the draught horses, with a distinctive long, low action.

Friesian

Used by German knights during the Crusades, this breed is now mostly a draught horse, very popular in its home in the northern Netherlands, although it can be a successful riding horse. Friesians are black with long-feathered fetlocks, making them look very impressive. They are popular for funeral hearses because of their black colour, and Harrods has a delivery van drawn by them.

Shire

The massive but gentle Shire holds a special place in the hearts of most horse lovers. Although Shires are no longer needed for ploughing the land, they are still popular and often take part in ploughing matches and are among the star attractions at many county shows. Recently, with the trend towards ever bigger riding horses, Shire crosses have become more common.

Suffolk Punch

The increasingly rare Suffolk Punch is various shades of chestnut with a flaxen mane and tail. Originally bred to be an all-round farm horse, the breed has declined in recent years. Prince Charles is a fan of the breed and uses them for working the land at Highgrove.

Registering Your Horse

If you are interested in buying a purebred horse, the chances are that the breeder will have registered it with the breed society at birth. Even if you don't buy from the breeder, any subsequent owner should have been given the registration certificate, so ask to see it when you try the horse. It will give you basic information about the horse's sire and dam, as well as its breeder. It will also have details on the horse's markings and its date of birth. Nowadays, of course, the horse passport, which is compulsory for all horses, will also give you information that helps you to track your horse's history.

When you buy a horse, the change of ownership must be registered with the issuer of the passport. It is usually optional to register as the new owner with the breed society, although most people like to do this.

Horse Colours

Many horse breeds have a limited range of recognized colours. For example, Friesians are always black, and skewbald and piebald are not accepted by the Dartmoor breed society – other breeds can be of almost any colour.

These are the basic horse colours:

- **Bay:** bay is a brown body with black points – mane, tail and legs up to the knee or hock.
- **Black:** it is rare to have a true black-coated horse; most are actually very dark brown. But a black horse is simply all black.
- **Brown:** body, points, mane, tail and legs are all brown.
- **Chestnut:** a light reddish-brown colour all over. The mane and tail may also be reddish-brown or lighter.
- **Liver chestnut:** a deep rich brown colour either all over or just in the coat, with the mane and tail being lighter.
- **Grey:** greys have a black skin and white hair, often with black hairs mixed in. Many greys begin life very dark grey or even black, and become lighter with age. Dapple greys have distinct circles of dark hair surrounding lighter grey hair all over their body. Fleabitten greys are mainly white-haired with small patches of hair of another colour – brown usually – throughout.
- **Roan:** roan is a base colour with white mixed evenly throughout the coat. Strawberry roan is a chestnut with white hairs, while blue roan is a black horse with white hairs.
- **Dun:** a creamy yellow to biscuit-brown coat colour with black points and often a black dorsal stripe.

- **Piebald and skewbald:** a piebald is a horse with large black and white patches all over its body. A skewbald has large patches of white and any other colour but black.

 Strictly speaking, palomino is simply a coat colour, but in America the breeding of palomino horses has long adhered to a certain standard, which has resulted in the production of high-standard palomino-coloured horses that can be registered with the Palomino Horse Breeders of America registry.

Above All Else, Enjoy Your Horse!

Owning a purebred horse puts you in touch with an equine community that shares many of your interests. People can get quite fierce in their devotion to a particular breed. But you certainly don't need to own a purebred to enjoy your horse – far from it. Maybe your horse is a cross between two breeds, in which case you can have fun learning about both and trying to pick out the characteristics of each that your horse exhibits. However, as long as she's healthy and has four good legs and feet, what breed she is will probably have little impact on your overall enjoyment of your horse.

CHAPTER 3

Anatomy

Knowing a little about how the horse is put together can help you understand when something is wrong and what the problem might be related to. Understanding the various systems can also help you understand proper equine management and avoid many problems.

The Teeth

Horses have two basic kinds of teeth: molars and incisors. Like most animals, the incisors are used for biting off things (such as grass), and the molars are used for grinding what they bite off before it goes through the rest of the digestive system.

FIGURE 3.1(a):
One year

FIGURE 3.1(b):
Five years

FIGURE 3.1(c):
Fifteen years

  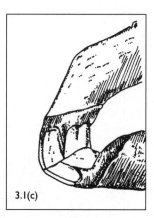

The foal will begin to show teeth within a couple weeks of birth. Between the ages of two and five years, baby teeth begin to shed and are replaced by permanent teeth.

The horse has at least 36 permanent teeth: 12 incisors at the front of the jaw, and 12 premolars and 12 molars at the back. Most horses also have four tiny wolf teeth. These grow just in front of the premolars on both jaws and are usually removed because they interfere with the bit. They have a shallow root so are quite easy to take out. Some horses, mostly males, also have tushes – small teeth just behind the incisors on both jaws.

Underbites and Overbites

Also known as sow mouth (underbite) or parrot mouth (overbite), these malocclusions of the incisors are genetically based (breeding stock with these problems should be gelded or not used as brood mares). The most pressing issue that these abnormalities cause is uneven wear, especially if the molars are also out of alignment.

Galvayne's Groove

This groove starts at the base of both the top and bottom teeth, making its first appearance at around 10 years of age. The groove grows out with the tooth and recedes off the bottom as the tooth elongates. At around the age of 30, the groove disappears from the tooth.

As much as 10cm (4in) of the horse's tooth is imbedded in the jawbone. The horse's teeth keep growing out from that base throughout its life.

Tooth Wear

If the molars wear unevenly, they can develop sharp edges. As a result, the horse will lose food out of his mouth, have difficulty chewing and perhaps even drool. Eventually, since he is not getting full nutritional benefit from his food, the horse will lose weight, because he is either dropping it or passing it through his system before it is fully digested.

The adult horse's teeth should be checked annually for proper wear. An equine dentist will examine the teeth both visually and manually, using a gag (speculum) to keep the mouth open. If he or she finds sharp edges from uneven wear, the dentist will rasp the teeth with special tools made specifically for horses (known as 'floating')and bring the teeth back to an even grinding surface again.

The Digestive System

Horses have a huge digestive system but a stomach capacity of only about 15l (3gal). The horse in the wild eats continually, passing food through its digestive tract all the time, emptying out the stomach and processing the food through to elimination.

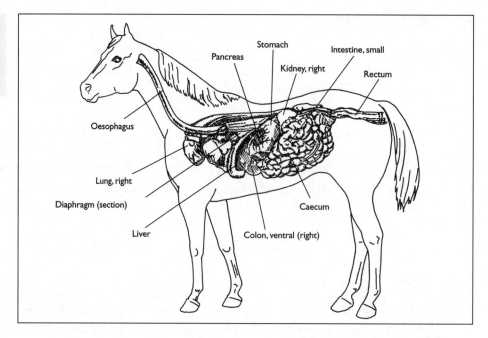

Domestic horses without access to pasture should have at least two and perhaps three hard feed meals per day, depending on the quantity they are receiving (which depends on the level of work that is required of them). Hay can be fed ad lib, if possible, but again, it is more likely to be split up into three or four batches a day. The main point is that the horse's digestive system is a large, complex machine that needs to be constantly processing food but not stuffed so full that it can't do its job properly.

The Mouth

As with all animals, digestion begins with the chewing process, reducing food material to a size and consistency more conducive to the remaining digestive process. For the horse, however, not much actual digestion takes place in the mouth, although the process does help produce the significant amounts of saliva needed for digestion.

The Oesophagus

This muscular tube is approximately 1.2m (4ft) long. It moves the food from the mouth to the stomach in rhythmic contractions. The oesophagus has a one-way valve at the entrance to the stomach that prevents the horse from vomiting.

The Stomach

The horse's relatively small stomach contains acid and pepsin, which break food down.

The Small Intestine

Approximately 21.2 m (70ft) long, the small intestine has around a 45l (9.5gal) capacity. Digested foods are absorbed and enter the bloodstream, while some are processed by the liver and stored as energy.

The Caecum

This critical apparatus contains a huge amount of bacteria. All ingested food passes through the caecum in a sort of side trip through the system. The bacteria break down cellulose (which the body cannot digest) and produce fat-soluble vitamins that are absorbed and used.

Smaller, frequent feedings are best, otherwise the stomach will move food before it is fully digested. This can mean that the horse isn't getting the full nutritional value of its feed, and also poses a greater risk of becoming impacted at one of those odd kinks and turns in the system.

The Large and Small Colons

The large colon has numerous parts (right lower, left lower, right upper, left upper and transverse) and is around 3.6m (12ft) long. It holds as much as 75.56l (15.8gal) of semiliquid stool. The small colon is a little shorter, at 3–3.6m (10–12ft) long; water is absorbed in it and stool is formed into balls.

The Rectum

Around 30.5cm (12in) long, this is the channel through which the stool leaves the body.

The Muscles

The horse has muscles in every part of its body. Short thick muscles provide short bursts of speed, and long lean muscles are needed for both speed and endurance.

FIGURE 3.3:
The muscles of
the horse

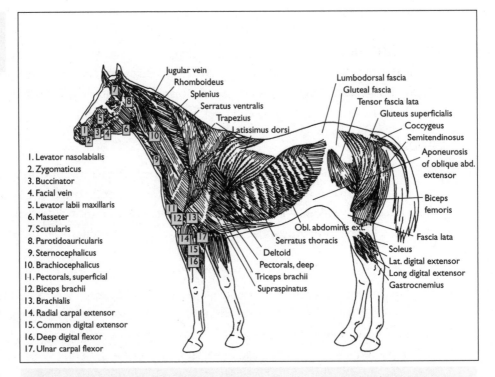

Jugular vein
Rhomboideus
Splenius
Serratus ventralis
Trapezius
Latissimus dorsi

Lumbodorsal fascia
Gluteal fascia
Tensor fascia lata
Gluteus superficialis
Coccygeus
Semitendinosus
Aponeurosis
of oblique abd.
extensor

Biceps
femoris

Fascia lata
Soleus
Lat. digital extensor
Long digital extensor
Gastrocnemius

Obl. abdomints ext.
Serratus thoracis
Deltoid
Pectorals, deep
Triceps brachii
Supraspinatus

1. Levator nasolabialis
2. Zygomaticus
3. Buccinator
4. Facial vein
5. Levator labii maxillaris
6. Masseter
7. Scutularis
8. Parotidoauricularis
9. Sternocephalicus
10. Brachiocephalicus
11. Pectorals, superficial
12. Biceps brachii
13. Brachialis
14. Radial carpal extensor
15. Common digital extensor
16. Deep digital flexor
17. Ulnar carpal flexor

The contraction of muscles causes the production of lactic acid. Muscle fatigue results when there is too much of a build-up of lactic acid, which causes a syndrome known as 'tying up'. Proper conditioning allows the horse to increase the muscles' ability to cope with lactic acid.

The Skeletal System

The horse's body is made up of 216 bones. The forelegs carry as much as 60 per cent of the weight of the horse. By understanding the skeletal system of the horse, you can better understand how the horse moves and how movement may be hindered or aided when riding. For instance, in the diagram, you can see the scapula, a huge bone at the shoulder just above and in front of the ribs. It isn't difficult to imagine that a saddle that rests too far forwards on the horse will interfere with movement of the shoulder structure.

FIGURE 3.4:
The skeletal system of the horse

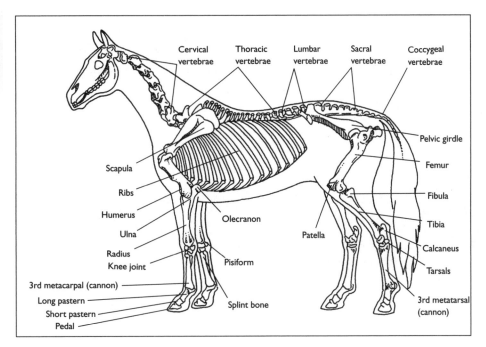

Listed below are some definitions relating to the bones. All these parts of the bone are highly subject to injury.

· **Periosteum** is the layer of dense connective tissue covering each bone.
· **Joint** is the union of two bones whose position is maintained by ligaments, tendons and a fibrous capsule.

- **Synovial membrane** is the connective tissue lining the inside of the joint.
- **Synovial fluid** allows for smooth movement of the joint.
- **Navicular bone** is a wedge-shaped bone in the foot that sits behind the coffin joint.
- **Bursae** are fluid-filled sacs between the tendons and the bones.

The Spine

The horse's spine is composed of 18 thoracic and six lumbar vertebrae.

Arthritis

Arthritis can be a significant problem for this athletic animal. The horse is inflicted with many specific arthritic conditions, including bone spavin (arthritis of the hock joint).

X-rays are used for arthritis diagnosis, and the typical treatment is pain-relieving medication and rest.

What does conformation mean?
The overall structure of the horse is known as its **conformation.** Few horses, if any, have perfect conformation. What is considered good conformation depends a great deal on what you plan to do with the horse.

The Foot

The horse's foot is a complex and extraordinary apparatus. It not only holds a great amount of weight but also is able to withstand high impact from that weight. The hoof of a mature horse grows approximately 8mm (^{5}/16in) a month. Proper trimming and shoeing by a good farrier when needed is critical to the horse's soundness.

FIGURE 3.5:
The foot of
the horse

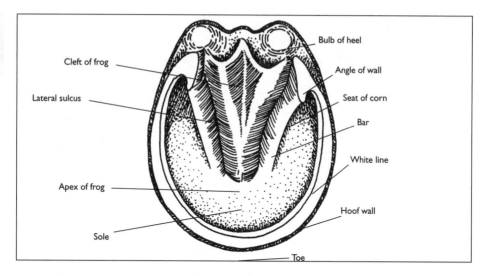

Bulb of heel
Cleft of frog
Angle of wall
Lateral sulcus
Seat of corn
Bar
White line
Apex of frog
Hoof wall
Sole
Toe

An interesting comparison can be made between the lower foreleg of the horse and the hand of the human:

- The knee or carpal joint in the horse corresponds to the human wrist.
- Everything below the horse's knee equals the bones of the human hand.
- Only three metacarpal bones are present in the horse (the cannon bone, splint bone and fetlock joint, which equals the human knuckle joint), as opposed to five in the human.
- The long pastern bone in the horse equals the proximal phalanx (the first bone in the finger).
- The outer insensitive laminae of the hoof corresponds to the fingernail in a human.

Horses have the unique ability to lock the stifle (see FIGURE 3.7), allowing them to relax the rest of their muscles and sleep while standing up, without the possibility of falling down. This is possible because the horse has three patella ligaments in the stifle.

Shock Absorption

Five factors make possible the shock absorption properties of the hoof:

1. The digital cushion found deep within the foot.
2. The hoof wall, which is the key structural support designed to take impact and spread it to the other shock-absorbing areas.
3. The sole, which is concave and therefore doesn't hit the ground.
4. The frog – a wedge of horn that is triangular in shape and presses into the digital cushion.
5. The bulbs of the heel, which form the back of the frog and the bars beside the frog.

Avoid any foot problems by arranging for a farrier to visit your horse on a regular basis. If your horse loses a shoe, she will feel very sensitive on that foot. Call the farrier immediately to prevent the hoof from becoming damaged. You might like to keep a rubber hoof boot handy to use if your horse does lose a shoe, and for treating foot problems.

Vision

The horse's visual capabilities are unique and well suited to her needs. The uniqueness of the horse's vision contributes considerably to the horse's reputation for spooking easily. The horse's eye is not round, and therefore the retina and cornea are not equidistant from each other across the eye. In order to focus on an object, the horse needs to turn her head and focus with both eyes.

Another contributing factor to the horse's tendency to spook is that the placement of the eyes on either side of the head makes the horse's vision largely monocular – she has one view of the world on the right side of her body and a different view on the left side. The horse can see as much as 350° around her body, with a blind spot directly in front and directly behind. This independent vision allows the horse to be on the lookout for predators while grazing.

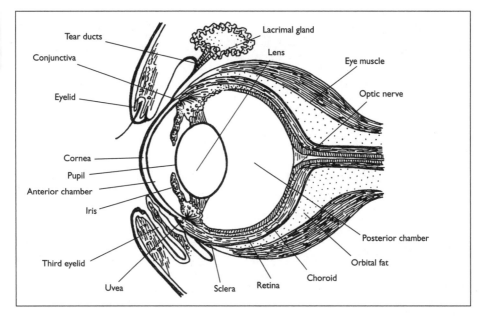

FIGURE 3.6:
The eye of
the horse

The eye diagram labels: Tear ducts, Conjunctiva, Eyelid, Lacrimal gland, Lens, Eye muscle, Optic nerve, Cornea, Pupil, Anterior chamber, Iris, Third eyelid, Uvea, Sclera, Retina, Choroid, Posterior chamber, Orbital fat

Well-Protected Eyes

Horses' eyes are surrounded by huge amounts of bone structure and set
in a layer of fat that allows the eye to push back into a cavity, which keeps
the eye well protected.

Problems

While the eye is well protected and eye problems are not prevalent, the
horse can have problems with the eye – some causing blindness – that are
similar to those of humans and other animals.

Conjunctivitis, an eye redness caused by irritated conjunctiva, is
perhaps the most common and simple eye problem you may encounter.
But a red eye can be the sign of a more serious disease, such as an ulcer, so
always be sure to check with your veterinarian.

The Respiratory System

The respiratory health of the horse is greatly affected by equine
management. Horses who spend a lot of time locked in closed stables are

subject to respiratory problems caused by constantly breathing urine odours and exposure to hay, indoor arenas, dusty oats and so on.

Don't forget respiratory conditioning if you are planning a specific activity for your horse. Such conditioning can occur by gradually increasing the periods of trotting.

COPD

Perhaps the most commonly known respiratory ailment is chronic obstructive pulmonary disease, known as COPD or sometimes called the heaves. This is a chronic problem usually caused by dust and mould in the feed. Many horses who develop COPD either need to have their hay soaked in water before eating it or be fed alternatives such as haylage or wilted grass.

Pneumonia

As with humans, pneumonia in horses is caused by virus, bacteria and foreign bodies in the lungs. Antibiotics may be administered, and rest is typically prescribed. Your veterinarian will be able to make this diagnosis.

Skin

The best way to avoid skin problems is to reduce the risks of broken skin (including lacerations from dangers in paddocks or stables, and abrasions from badly fitting equipment) and to put into place a solid equine management programme to reduce parasite exposure.

Miniature pilorector muscles connect to the roots of the long hair of the horse's coat. When it is cold and these muscles contract, the long hairs stand up straight and trap air, which provides insulation. In winter, good grooming helps keep the coat free from mud that mats the hair and lessens its ability to perform this function.

The Skin's Job

The skin of the horse has all the same jobs as the skin of any animal:

· It provides a barrier against foreign objects.
· It serves as a huge sensory organ.

· It synthesizes vitamins.
· It provides insulation.

The Layers of the Skin

The skin has two main layers – the epidermis and the dermis – as well as a layer of fat just below its surface. Regular grooming helps the horse maintain a healthy hair coat by removing dirt and matted material and by increasing the production of sebum, an oily substance that helps the horse shed water and makes the coat shine.

FIGURE 3.7:
The parts of
the horse

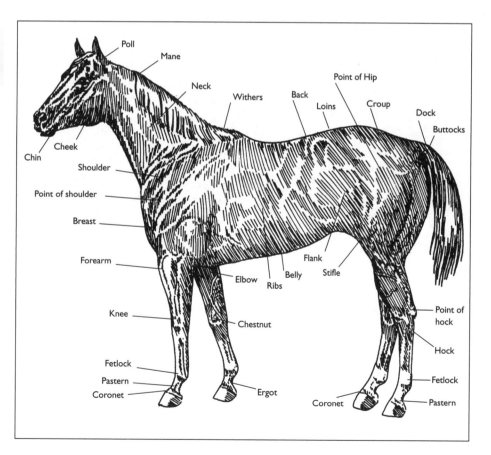

Knowledge is Key

It would take several lifetimes to know and understand all the information that is currently available about the horse. However, take the time to learn at least the basics about how your horse operates. This knowledge will enable you to make better management decisions and help keep your horse fit, healthy and ready to ride.

CHAPTER 4

Horse Behaviour

Your horse's behaviour is perhaps the most important thing for you to understand and influence for the two of you to be able to have a satisfying relationship. How your horse behaves around you and in the stable yard is the key to your safety, as well as that of your horse and everyone who interacts with her.

Wild Herd Behaviour

Horses are herd animals. In its simplest description, this means that in the wild, they would survive by roaming in groups. But herds are quite complex. They consist mostly of mares, called harem bands, who are serviced by one stallion who protects and defends the herd. The patriarch is the sole adult male horse in the herd; all the other males are young colts who will be driven out to live in a 'bachelor band' when they are mature enough to become interested in breeding and represent a threat to the patriarch's harem.

There are also young fillies in the herd, who will remain with the herd until they are either stolen by a stallion trying to start or increase his harem band, or are bred within the harem by their own father or by a new stallion who takes over the herd, which happens, on average, every two to three years.

What is the flehman response?
The curling of the upper lip by a male horse in response to the scent of a female is referred to as the **flehman response**.

The dominant member of the herd, however, is a mare. This mare decides where the herd goes and, as the high-ranking member, gets first choice of food and water. Through a process of testing and retesting, all members of the herd will have come to understand and accept this as standard. If a member of the herd does not submit to the lead mare, the lead mare excommunicates the horse from the herd, driving him or her outside the group and leaving the horse vulnerable to predators and to finding its own food. The horse may learn and be accepted back; join a bachelor band if it's a stallion; or be scooped up by another stallion's harem if it's a mare.

In domestic horse life, stallions have the reputation for being dangerous and wanting what they want – which tends to be to mate with any mare in sight – whether or not there's a human being in the way. But anyone who has had mares knows that little compares with the bossiness of a mare, and that it makes sense that a lead mare would boss the herd around most of the time.

The stallion keeps the herd together, and newcomers are not allowed into the established herd without the stallion's OK. With the mare and stallion dominating, all other members of the herd are part of a pecking order. As the herd dynamic changes – members die, foals are born and youngsters age – the pecking order constantly adjusts. Age typically determines rank, with the youngsters being at the bottom, but as they grow older, these young horses constantly challenge and, thus, alter the status quo. In his book *Influencing Horse Behaviour*, Dr Jim McCall puts it rather eloquently: 'In the herd, the submissive must show respect to the dominant. The young must not invade the personal space of the elders. Higher ranking members of the herd are not to be ignored. Herd laws are consistent within all equine herds, only the individuals are different. This consistency gives the horse a sense of harmony. He knows how he fits into his world.'

Domestic Herd Behaviour

There are few 'natural' herds in this country, but if you have more than one horse or keep your horse at a stable with other horses, you will have ample opportunity to see horse-to-horse behaviour in action. Of course, the domestic 'herd' dynamic is somewhat different from that of a wild herd. In the wild, the herd grows and changes according to breeding season, and there is a natural mix of younger and ageing animals. In your yard, the 'herd' changes artificially, directed by humans according to a horse being sold or a new arrival, and newcomers to the herd are often of similar age, size or even the same sex as the existing herd members.

Nonetheless, watching groups of domestic horses interact can be the most fascinating part of being around horses. I could spend hours watching my three – an 11-year-old gelding, an eight-year-old mare and a four-year-old filly – sort things out in the course of their day together. The mare and gelding have lived together since the mare was six months old. The filly came into the picture when the mare was six; my mare has had a lot to say to the newcomer. The gelding just assumes the others know he's the elder statesman, and he occasionally lifts a leg or pins back his ears as a reminder that nothing has changed, especially when one of the others thinks she might like to eat out of his hay pile. And that's just the tip of the conversational iceberg that takes place among these three throughout the entire day. Who gets to drink, who runs down the hill from the back field first, what position he or she takes when they get there, and how close they get to stand to each other are all under discussion, especially since the filly is constantly challenging her place in the arrangement.

Self-Preservation

The horse's instinct for self-preservation can easily control its behaviour to a point that seems self-destructive. But it is so highly ingrained that the horse cannot help but listen to that nagging feeling if something seems to be threatening its very survival. The behaviour a horse exhibits when concerned with its own survival can be very hard to understand.

Learning about horse behaviour and looking for the underlying reason from the horse's point of view can be fascinating and rewarding for both human and horse.

A friend who breeds horses once had a yearling colt who, shortly after he was weaned, began to be more and more wary of my friend. The colt was in with a couple of other foals of his age, who were as friendly as all the other youngsters she'd raised over the years. Finally, she presented this horse and its growing problem to a horse trainer who was giving a clinic at her farm. He described the horse as having such a high degree of self-preservation instinct that things seemed threatening to him that didn't really bother most other horses. He showed the group watching him work with the colt how he would present himself to this horse and begin to change his behaviour, teaching the young horse that he was a trustworthy human and not a threat. The trainer explained that most horses are so sensitive that they can understand when you mean them no harm, but that this particular horse's self-preservation instinct was so highly developed that it ruled over his other sensitivities.

My friend expressed concern that many people would have instantly decided this horse had been abused. Yet I have known her for years, and the only 'abuse' her animals get is an overdose of kindness!

Turning Horses Out Together

There is no denying that horse play can be very boisterous, which is why people are often reluctant to let horses be loose together. Domestic horses, like wild horses, will establish a pecking order, and in determining their ranks, the scene can get a little wild, with biting, kicking, charging, rearing and other potentially harmful actions. Yes, horses can definitely hurt each other. But feral horses roaming in a 'wild' state almost never injure each other – it is the domestic arrangement in which we keep horses that makes injury much more possible.

Horses would rather not be hurt, and most horses will wisely pay attention to each other's subtle signals and know when to avoid actual physical contact. A horse turned out with an established group of other horses will be completely aware at all times, reading the messages that the other horses are sending and acting accordingly. One would think that this alone would be enough to ensure that you can put horses together at any time without them hurting each other. But there are at least two things that humans do that mess up this natural order of things.

Not Enough Space

When turned out alone, horses should always have the absolute maximum space that you can carve out for them. However, when putting horses out together, a great amount of space is even more important. It never ceases to amaze me how far my mare will chase my filly to let her know where her real boundary line is. If the horse being chased has nowhere to go but over or through the fence to get out of the situation, that is where the horse will go. But if there is ample space, then the lower-echelon horse has room to learn the lesson of boundaries and won't get hurt in the process.

Imprinting is a specific desensitizing (and controversial) method used with a newborn foal. An American vet, Robert Miller, DVM, has spent years developing the theory and technique of imprinting with horses. His technique involves handling the newborn foal extensively to accustom it to events it will encounter later in life. Imprinting is only as successful as the skill and knowledge of the person using it. Decide for yourself whether imprinting is right for your horses by reading Dr Miller's book *Imprint Training of the Newborn Foal.*

Some horses don't put on a chase like my mare does, but instead may back up and kick with both back feet at their opponent or lunge with bared teeth. If the space is big enough and there are no corners and small passages to get trapped in, the horse getting the worse end of the deal can stay out of reach of teeth or hind feet. But if the space is too small, the horse can easily be pinned in a corner and kicked badly. If given enough space, a horse's choice will almost always be to get out of the way as requested. If the ample space they are in is a grassy pasture, most horses are too occupied with their nose in the grass to spend much time getting in arguments anyway!

Socializing Horses

Horse owners often make the choice to never put their horse in with another horse, for fear that they will hurt each other. Although this choice is understandable, a solitary life is, I think, very unfair to the horse. Horses crave companionship and interaction with their own kind. Even though they surely have some innate knowledge of the meaning of signals given off by other horses, the unsocialized horse often doesn't understand pecking order and the seriousness of the signals.

Frequently horses hurt one another because two or more horses are suddenly thrown together. If just one of them is unaccustomed to being with other horses, problems will develop quickly. For example, if an unsocialized horse walks over to the hay pile of another horse, the horse with possession of the hay, Ms Dominant, will pin back her ears, cock a leg or give some other threat that says 'I'm boss, this is my hay pile, and I'm not sharing'. The unsocialized horse is not likely to understand dominant and submissive standings in the herd and, therefore, won't understand what the signals mean. If he keeps coming closer, a bigger reaction is likely to follow. When this happens, one of the horses could get hurt. And thus the cycle continues, because, of course, when people hear of events such as this, they are even less inclined to put horses together.

Horses at hacking stables are usually pretty well socialized, but they often haven't learned to control their actions when around humans. A dangerous situation can develop when, for example, a novice rider doesn't understand the warning signals that the horse is giving to another about following too closely. A good kick from the front horse can result, so always keep safe distances between horses.

Introducing Horses to Each Other

The best time to socialize horses is when they are young. When young, they love to play, and do so mostly without seriously hurting each other. At the same time, they learn to read each other's signals and coexist peacefully. Of course, the mare will have taught her youngster some things, but that doesn't always translate into understanding the same signals from a horse that is not his mother. And a horse who has learned only from his mother may not know that it can be hurt, since the mare would typically not do anything to really hurt her offspring.

A horse that is well socialized will more easily be able to get along with a new horse or group of horses. But even then, to be fair to your horse, you should put it with other horses who are socialized as well. When I temporarily moved to a new area, I kept my mare at a large livery yard. After she had settled in for a couple of days, I was happy with her being turned out with a group of other horses. The pastures and turnouts were large enough, and none of the horses looked exceptionally banged up. My mare was well socialized, and I knew from watching her in the past that she was very good at avoiding trouble with other horses. The horses at this yard clearly were well socialized and were given the chance to live artificially like a 'herd', even for just part of the day.

When I bring a new horse home, I blend it into the established 'herd' gradually over the course of at least four stages: I let them see one another, put them side by side in paddocks, put the new horse out with one other horse, and put the group together. I don't care how many days or weeks this takes, as I size up how each seems to be reacting to the other and move to the next stage accordingly. Here are the steps I recommend:

1. First, put the horse in an enclosure where there is no common fence line with the other horses. (I use my round pen, which I don't use for everyday turnout.) That way, everyone gets to see and hear the newcomer, and the newcomer gets to check out its surroundings without the potential problem of breaking fences and getting hurt in the process.

2. After the yelling at each other and racing around, the horses usually settle down in a day or two, and the second step is to move the new horse to a paddock adjacent to the existing herd. My paddock has an electric fence around the wooden fences – mostly to keep the horses from chewing the wood all day – that helps keep them from getting too friendly over the fence. But it is still open enough for the horses to touch noses, squeal and do all the other things they like to do for introductions, without being able to actually strike each other. If the horses are stabled at night, add the step of putting the new horse beside one of the horses she will eventually be turned out with, preferably in stables where they can at least see each other; this gives them more chance to get accustomed to each other from a distance.

3. When they've settled down and can ignore each other, which usually takes a day or two, it's time to put at least a couple of them together. If the new horse is going to join an existing herd of more than one other horse, pull all of the old residents out into other paddocks or stables for an afternoon or two, and let the newcomer and just one horse get accustomed to each other. This really all depends on how they have acted thus far and what the personalities of the existing herd members are like.

4. Finally, when you do put them all together, set out piles of hay at a good distance apart to give them something else to preoccupy themselves with besides each other. This can work like a charm – by the time they finish

the hay pile, they look up and say, 'Hey, it's you, the horse I've seen over the fence for a few days', and go off and have a drink or doze in the sun.

Inevitably they will check each other out, and some squealing and maybe even some striking and a little biting may go on. Typically, this sounds a whole lot worse than it actually is – they seem to wait until the second you walk around the corner of the barn to squeal and grunt at each other. You run back expecting to see slices of horse flesh hanging from one of the horse's mouths, but what you find is the two offenders looking at you and apparently wondering why you suddenly reappeared.

If after a couple of days, two of the group just won't leave each other alone, you may have to separate them or work on some new groupings.

Horses, like other animals, communicate by making a range of sounds. These include:

- **Snort and/or blowing sound:** horses tend to make a snorting noise – sometimes a short snort and at other times an elongated sound – when they are afraid of something. This seems to make the horse appear even larger and more impressive to the potential danger.
- **Nicker:** this low, friendly rat-tat-tat-tat sound is one that horses use as a greeting.
- **Neigh/whinny:** high-pitched, long and loud, a whinny is another greeting that can be used for long distances.
- **Squeal:** This somewhat unpleasant, short, high-pitched sound is the one you'll hear when two horses are getting to know each other.
- **Scream:** This sound happens in a true fight, often between competing stallions – something that we rarely witness in domesticated horse life.

Grouping by Age

Although this is rarely done, grouping by age range is much more logical than grouping by sex. Putting a very young horse – a horse under two years old – in with a group of older horses can have bad results. Youngsters can get hurt just because of their size differences. After the age of two or three, most horses tend to be of substantial size compared to adults and are a little less delicate. If at all possible, and at the very least, make sure that a young horse has a couple of companions of similar age in the group.

Horses may seem 'stupid' to the general public because they are known to exhibit fear of things such as rocks or a piece of paper blowing in the wind. My response to people who tell me that horses are stupid is that horses think and make decisions like horses. We humans smoke cigarettes despite dire health warnings, and are reported in the newspapers for murdering each other for the change in our pockets. So who are we to call horses stupid?

The Stallion Dilemma

Of course, stallions present a different issue altogether, and clearly cannot run with mares with whom you do not want them to breed. Well-behaved stallions can be run with geldings, but this is not always the best solution.

A Word of Caution

Keep in mind that this information represents guidelines and ideas that are based on what I or others have tried and found to work in grouping horses. There is always a situation that defies all rules of thumb – the horse living alone that actually prefers it that way; the foal who lives with a group of aged geldings and gets along well; or the horse that gets seriously injured in what had been for months a 'perfect' grouping of horses. With horses, the unexpected does happen, and ultimately you are the decision-maker when it comes to your horse.

Domestic horses are products of their environment and of whatever education they have received from humans. Their 'education' is not just specific 'training', but occurs every moment that a human interacts with them, from riding to grooming to just picking manure out of the paddock when the horse is in it.

Maybe your horse deserves a nice rub around the ears after a workout. But instead of him pushing against you as if you're a post, maybe it would be a little nicer for both of you if Rubby could look forward to a gentle grooming around the head and ears with a towel and a nice soft brush. And make sure you are doing the rubbing. The horse doesn't need to rub back; he can just relax and enjoy the attention. Let him rub later on the tree out in his pasture if he wants to.

Even if you've been giving your horse the wrong message all these years – if he's been rummaging around your pockets and nipping at you, flinging off the halter and rushing off to the food bucket, knocking you out of the way to get to the hay pile, or moving off before you are even mounted and settled in the saddle – it's never too late to start teaching new messages! Although it's going to be harder to undo what has been done, horses are pretty clever and can learn new things if you perfect your ability to teach them. It's entirely up to you.

Learning the Signals

After observing horses and how they interact with each other, you can begin to understand some of the early signals that a horse might be giving. In other words, the horse almost always does something first that serves as a signal to the approaching action. World-class horseman Ray Hunt has a now-famous line: 'What happened before what happened happened?' That's the place you want to learn to be aware of. Before a horse can kick out with a hind leg, it almost always has to shift its weight off the leg it plans to kick with. If you learn to be aware of the weight shift, you will never have to worry about the kick. There's even likely to be a step before that weight shift, such as a glance with ears slightly pinned back. You can make good use of increased awareness in both handling and riding horses. Remember: horses are experts at not expending any more energy than necessary, so they will almost certainly give you some signals. It's up to you to pick up on them.

Leading by Respect, not Fear

Horses naturally look for a leader to tell them how things are. It is the way of the herd. In the horse/human relationship, it makes sense for the human to be the leader. Everyone stays a little safer that way, since sometimes what a horse thinks is the best idea – for example, to bolt for home across that major road – often isn't in the best interest of both parties. (Of course, sometimes the human's idea isn't in the best interest of both parties either, but that is the topic for another book.)

Clever Hans was an Arab stallion in Berlin in the early 20th century, whose schoolmaster owner, Wilhelm von Osten, taught him to solve mathematical equations, answer geography questions, identify musical scores and do other things that we don't associate with a horse's normal range of knowledge. A test was eventually conducted that determined that von Osten was giving signals to Clever Hans from a spot behind the horse. Unless you knew that horses can see almost completely behind them, you wouldn't have guessed that this was taking place.

Being the leader doesn't have to preclude having a partnership with your horse. And it definitely doesn't mean that you have to establish a relationship with your horse that is based on fear – in fact, that is exactly what you don't want. A horse can follow its leader either out of fear or out of respect, and to the novice horse handler, the outcome of either of these approaches may look the same, but are actually quite different. Of course, I advocate gaining your horse's respect; to me, the lives, thoughts and feelings of animals are no less valuable than those of humans. And you can feel that way about horses and still not let them walk all over you.

Some horses are natural leaders themselves; they can be the most challenging and the most interesting to work with. If you are a beginner, you will probably want to get some help with such horses. These horses seem to think, 'Well, if this human isn't going to be the leader, then I am.' A horse who seems a bit of a rogue in the hands of a beginner can be a gentle horse when handled by an experienced horse person.

To Move or be Moved

Horses decide the position of other horse herd members and human members of their herd according to who the 'movers' are. Higher-ranking herd members do not need to exert much effort to get lower-ranking herd mates to move out of their space (or to not move into it) – ears back or a leg barely raised can be enough.

If dominance is determined by who does the moving, the human needs to be the mover, not the moved. This is not easy – every interaction you have with your horse presents an opportunity to be moved. You always need to be aware of this, even when you are just going into your horse's paddock to fill the water trough.

I'm not suggesting that you need to be *aggressive* with your horse, but you may need to learn to be *assertive*. Pay attention to where your horse is when you enter his space and what he does as you interact with him. For instance, a common reaction of a young horse on a lead rope who is learning to be led and move around you respectfully is to drop his shoulder into you and push you out of his way if he is confused by what you want. This is the kind of thing you need to nip in the bud. If you move a step back when your horse drops his shoulder, he has learned a big lesson about his ability to move you. The horse with the type of personality that will take advantage of this kind of experience will present you with all kinds of related behaviour to deal with. Even the most submissive horse will remember that he can simply move you out of the way when a real crisis comes up. (See Chapter 11.)

If you watch a horse signal another horse to not get near a particular pile of hay, for example, the first thing she might do is pin back her ears a little and jerk her head at the other horse. Socialized horses know those early signals – and they will either continue and challenge the horse for her pile or, more probably, move off. After a few times, the horse protecting the hay pile will only have to pin back her ears while still eating or lift her head, and the other horse will know that today is not a good day to share hay. You can learn to recognize signals (for example, the drop in the shoulder or, eventually, even a look in her eye) and then redirect the horse from that potential action before she actually follows through.

How to be Safe in the Group

Imagine that you have safely integrated your horse with the others at the yard and you now need to cope with the group as a whole, for example at feeding time.

If you feed the horses altogether in the field, you are going to have problems with fighting over food bowls and heaps of hay. I prefer to bring my horses in for meals, which means they can all eat in peace. But if this is not possible, you could consider the following:

- The pecking order system will be in action at feeding time, especially about hard feed. The safest thing to do would be to set up your feeding area so that you can feed them without going in with the group. You are better off not being accidentally in the line of fire when Jester tells Bumble for the umpteenth time that he eats from the third bucket from the barn wall. If you have to go in with the group and it is a little unruly, carry a flag (a long pole with a piece of cloth attached to one end and a comfortable handle on the other) or something that can help them learn that you are not to be mauled at feeding time.
- You will need to either spread hay far enough apart so that one horse doesn't guard three piles, or use a manger large enough for the number of horses you have – and large enough to provide the appropriate space they will need to eat it from the same place!

Ultimately, you need to set up your feeding space in as safe a way as possible. And you may want to consider those times when you need to get someone else to feed the horses. I prefer to set up my place so that no one who is unfamiliar with my horses and my handling preferences has to go in with my horses and interact with them while they are loose. Instead, the feeder can do almost everything from the other side of the fence.

The Homesick Horse

Because horses are herd animals and territory is important to them, most are bothered by being separated from their group or taken away from the yard. Some horses exhibit this displeasure so subtly that only the most experienced horse handler would even notice it. Others exhibit it so graphically that you can't help but notice – for instance, when you are being mowed down by a distraught horse dancing around on the end of a lead rope screaming for its friend, or when you are on a runaway horse who comes to a screeching halt only when he reaches his stable.

The chances are that you'll experience something somewhere in between, and you might even attribute the behaviour to another cause. Don't be fooled – the horse who plods along on the ride away from the yard but 'jogs' on the ride home is not suddenly fizzy for no reason.

The way to deal with this sort of behaviour will come up in the chapter on handling, but the important thing is to learn to offer your horse the support she needs in order to be comfortable with you while away from her equine friends. She needs to know that you are nice to be with, that you have a keen sense of her need for a pecking order, and that when things aren't looking so good, she doesn't need to race back to the yard but can turn to you to help her through it.

In order to succeed in getting your horse to have this kind of faith in you, you need to learn to be totally consistent, completely unwavering and infinitely reliable in your support and in the boundaries that you establish. You need to understand what is happening when this kind of behaviour arises. Instead of being convinced by well-meaning advice to turn to new and bigger bits or changes in feeding programmes, get to the root of the problem and up the level of your relationship with your horse a notch.

Stable Vices

Stable vices are basically bad habits that horses typically develop from being left in a confined area for too long. People think that confined horses are bored, and to counter their boredom, they hang toys in their stables or give them balls to play with. Horses, in my humble opinion, do not get bored in the way that people do. Horses develop stable vices not because they are bored but because they are frustrated and stressed about being confined; confinement is completely against their natural way of existing. They are large animals with nomadic lifestyles. They need to move that big body of theirs around at will. Horses who roam freely most of the time and get ridden regularly actually seem to enjoy some time snuggled up in a nicely bedded stable. Here are some of the common stable vices:

- **Windsucking:** this is perhaps the most insidious, most well-known and worst stable vice. When a horse windsucks, it grips its top front teeth on a hard edge, usually the top of a stable door or a fence board, pulls back and makes a grunting noise – and it does this over and over and over again. This is addictive behaviour that, once learned, is usually never stopped but can sometimes be controlled. The addiction has been discovered to come from a release of natural stress-relieving endorphins that the horse experiences each time it does this.
- **Crib-biting:** this is similar to windsucking, but rather than making the grunting noise, the horse tends to chew away bits of wood or whatever material he is biting.

Horses can learn to windsuck or crib-bite accidentally, or they can learn from the horse in the next stable or in their paddock with them. Such vices can be costly – when a 500kg (1,100lb) horse pulls back on something, whatever it is, it can cause a lot of damage. They can also affect the horse's health; for example, the front teeth will be worn unnaturally. And some horses are more interested in their addiction than in eating.

Some people don't mind having a horse with these vices, but if you are in the market for a horse, I suggest you avoid getting one. (Although the vices don't affect riding at all, they are technically considered an unsoundness, and anyone selling a horse is obliged to tell you about these habits.) If you keep your horse at livery and notice a horse nearby windsucking or crib-biting, get your horse moved out of that horse's sight (and preferably earshot).

If you have a horse that windsucks or crib-bites, or yours develops the habit, keep it outside all the time in an environment where there is little to practise on – electric fencing instead of wooden fencing; feed buckets loose on the ground, not attached to walls; a shelter that has no edges inside for the horse to grab onto, and so on. Be warned: the most addicted horses will find amazing ways to satisfy their addiction.

There are anti-crib collars available; they need to be adjusted perfectly and seem to be effective.

What is meant by sound and unsound?
If a horse is perfectly healthy, it is said to be **'sound'**. If a horse is temporarily lame or has some health problems, it is considered **'unsound'**. Anything that adversely affects a horse's health is considered an 'unsoundness'. If the horse's problem is chronic, the horse is 'permanently unsound'.

· **Weaving:** this is typically seen in a horse in a stable. The horse stands at the door and swings its head back and forth, back and forth, shifting its weight from one front leg to the other. This uneasy type of horse doesn't take confinement well. The problem will escalate if he develops any lameness issues that require immobility, because weaving is almost impossible to control physically. So if your horse starts to weave, you need to get the horse into a better frame of mind.
· **Digging/pawing:** this habit is as much annoying as it is anything else, although it can cause uneven foot wear for unshod horses on hard ground.

Encouraging Good Behaviour

When you earn a horse's trust, you have earned a lot. However, once you have it, you can't ever betray that trust – it's hard, but the minute you let someone talk you into trying that bigger bit or whatever, you jeopardize your horse's faith that you are consistent and trustworthy. Go with your good instincts, and if you feel unsure, enlist the aid of people whose instincts are similar to yours. This doesn't mean you should avoid exploring new ideas. However, using your good instincts as a guide will help to reinforce your horse's trust in you.

It is a sad fact (to humans) that our horses don't love us. They prefer to build their relationships around trust and respect. Therefore, you need to make sure that you aren't the submissive member of the partnership. Above everything else, your horse needs to know that he can rely on you when he's scared or concerned.

The behaviour of a horse that does not trust you can look pretty ugly, and yet the horse is not to blame. Find some mentors in the horse world who you can turn to before you reach the point where you can't handle your own horse. A trusting, respectful horse in the hands of a trustworthy, respectful human is wonderful to behold – and even more wonderful to experience.

CHAPTER 5

A Horse of Your Own

Now that you've had an overview of the different breeds of horses to choose from, know a little bit about the anatomy and physiology of these large and complicated animals and have some insight into their behaviour, it's time to get a horse of your own! However, I hope you read this entire book before you start looking seriously.

There are many places to find horses for sale and many different circumstances under which to buy them, the main ones being privates sales and sales from dealers and at auctions. You will hear as many good stories as bad stories about each way of buying a horse, but there are some places that are better than others for a beginner to look.

Deciding What You Want

Before you start looking, you should make a short list of some traits you would like in the horse you are planning to buy.

Age

A rule of thumb for a beginner is to stay away from horses under four or five years old. In reality, there are lots of horses between three and five who are a lot better educated than many horses in their teens and who are probably a lot safer for a beginner, but such youngsters have been handled and started under saddle by very reputable people who work with horses at a deep level. You need to know who you are dealing with to trust a youngster to be a safe bet for a beginner.

Between five and ten years old, many horses seem to gain some natural mellowing (although this is far from always the case!), and this usually means that the horse has simply had more experiences. But, ultimately, age is not the biggest factor for determining a horse's safety. There is a saying that a horse will eventually rise up or come down to the level of her rider/handler; many 20-plus-year-old horses are happy to run away with an unskilled rider if they feel unsupported in scary situations (which can include something as basic as leaving the yard).

The racehorse Red Rum holds a special place in the hearts of many horse-lovers and racegoers. This charismatic horse is the only one to have won the Grand National at Aintree three times – in 1973, 1974 and 1977. He died at the age of 30 in 1995 and is buried next to the winning post at Aintree. To find out more about Red Rum and other famous horses, go to *www.equinenet.org/heroes*.

History

Even young horses may have passed through numerous hands. Find out what you can about how many owners the horse has had, and about the circumstances of each sale. The horse's current seller may not know much, or may not offer much of what he or she does know, in order not to dampen your enthusiasm for the horse, but it's worth asking. Having too many owners can cause behaviour problems in horses, simply from having been handled inconsistently – or the horse may have changed hands often specifically because of behaviour problems.

Education

One of the most important things for you to know about your prospective horse is its level of education. Find out, if you can, who educated the horse as a youngster and who started him under saddle. How did it go? Who took care of the horse's education from there? And how was the horse educated? Was it trained with whips and spurs? Was it trained in the mechanical but effective approach of conditioned response? Or was it educated through a style of horsemanship in which the horse's natural instincts are used to the rider's advantage and the horse is taught through respect, not fear? Can you follow through with the method? If the horse will stop only if you yank on the bit, are you prepared to do this? Or, better still, are you prepared to spend the time and money for someone to re-educate the horse with you?

Colour

How important is colouring? It may not be a good reason to buy a particular horse, but let's face it – it matters. Some people are attracted to coloured horses and collect them for their colour alone. It does help to like the colour of the horse you'll look at every day, but when you finally find the horse whose temperament and education fits you, you won't even notice if it has pink polka dots.

Size

Again, size doesn't have to matter, but it can. Most people with large builds like to have a horse of some substance under them. A tall person typically would like the horse to be tall, too. Short people can go either way. But a beginner rider who is short can gain a lot of confidence on a smaller horse – believe me, it *is* further to the ground from a tall horse than a short one!

Conformation

Buying a horse that is well put together makes a lot of other things easier too, such as shoeing and saddle fitting. Although you learned some basic information on conformation and anatomy in Chapter 3, this is where an experienced horse person can really help you out. If you already have an idea that there is something specific you plan to do with the horse – such as jumping, dressage or gymkhana games – look for conformation specifics that might help the horse in that activity. Any horse is suitable to do almost any of these things for fun, but if you intend to compete, your equine athlete needs to have some innate ability in your chosen event.

Cost

Maybe this comes first in your case, or maybe your price range is wide enough that it is less of a priority. It is probable, though, that you have a top limit of how much you can spend on a horse. Although there are some market standards, these are pretty loose – what you consider a trait that should bring the price of a horse down may be of no consequence to the seller. The seller will have his or her own reasons for setting a price, including how much they have invested in the horse for things such as training. Expect to spend from nothing to £5,000 for your first horse, with anything in between being fair game. If your top price is £2,000, for example, there are many horses out there for you; it might just take a little longer to find the right one.

Where to Buy Horses

Now that you have a general description in mind of the horse you are looking for, it's time to start looking around.

Classified Ads

If you live in a horsey part of the country, you may find a lot of horses for sale in the classified section of the daily newspaper. If that isn't the case where you live, you won't get very far with a newspaper. However, you can find classified listings in any of the horsey magazines. 'Free ad' papers usually have a horse section. These papers are usually published locally; they are free to advertise in, and are either free or cost about £1.50–£2.00 to buy. They are a good place to start looking for your dream horse, as they will contain adverts for horses in your area, whereas horsey magazines tend to cover the whole country. Keep your horse-to-be profile in mind as you read the listings, and circle any that come close. Don't make calls on horses that don't fit one of the major points in your profile; this just wastes your time and money, as well as the time of the person who is selling the horse.

If you are well-connected in the local horse community, you may come across horses that are being given away. Many are given away because they have frightened their owners, or because the owner no longer has time or interest in riding, has tried to sell the horse without success and feels badly that the horse is just hanging around. Just remember: horses are never given away because they are *too* well-educated or too well-behaved.

Most of the time the horses listed in the classifieds are privately owned and being sold by owners of one or two horses. You'll need to travel around your area a bit, but this is a very legitimate and worthwhile way to look for a horse.

Here are some phrases you may run across in the classified ads:

· **Brood mare only:** a brood mare is a mare that has soundness problems that prevent her from being ridden but don't prevent her from being used for breeding.

- **Companion horse only:** this horse cannot be ridden and its only use would be to keep the grass down or keep another horse company.
- **Easy to do:** this generally means a horse that is well-behaved and quiet in the field and stable, and is easy to look after, not requiring any special treatment.
- **Green:** typically this means the horse has had a saddle on and tolerates being ridden, but hasn't had many hours under saddle.

What is a schoolmaster or schoolmistress?
A schoolmaster or schoolmistress is a nice, calm horse that tolerates inconsistent riding, tends to take care of its rider, and is a horse you would be comfortable with as a beginner or part-time rider. If you're lucky, such a horse will also be well-educated and know how to jump and do basic schooling exercises.

- **Needs bringing on:** this usually describes a horse who has been taught the fundamentals and is probably further along than 'green', but is still in the advanced beginner stage of its education as a riding horse.
- **Prospect:** this is a horse that the owner feels has the potential to excel in a particular type of activity if it is educated to do so.
- **Seen hounds:** the horse has been hunted. Remember, this doesn't tell you how it reacted when it saw the quarry!
- **Will go far in the right hands:** this horse's current owners think the horse has potential. It may have displayed some ability to jump or do dressage, but this is no guarantee that it can or ever will do these things well.
- **Willing over fences:** this horse has been jumped successfully (that is, it doesn't tend to balk).

Breeders

If you are interested in a specific breed of horse, you will definitely want to visit reputable breeders in your area. If you go further afield, you should factor in transport costs. Buying from a breeder may be a bit more expensive than some other sources of horses, but what you get if you go to reputable people is the best selection of top-quality horses. Breeders often have young animals because, logically, they breed and sell the offspring. But many breeders, in order to keep a wide selection, sell on commission other people's horses within their chosen breed. You should bring someone more experienced than you are with you to a breeder, since breeders are professionals and experts, and it's important to understand what they are telling and showing you.

Auctions

There is probably a horse auction taking place somewhere near you on an average of once a month or so. Check the local papers and horsey magazines. Horse auctions work like most auctions – people bring their horses, a professional auctioneer sells them, and a percentage goes to the auction house. The horse is led and/or ridden in front of the audience, and the highest bidder wins. Usually there are contingencies for vet checks and for you to test ride the horse, but you need to know these details before you hold up your bidder's number. If this method of buying a horse interests you at all, you should plan to visit a few auctions before considering buying. It is possible to buy wonderful horses this way, but you need to have some experience or fully trust your advisor, as some horses for sale can be equally dreadful.

Dealers

Dealers are in the business of buying and selling horses. They are usually not breeders and do not breed their own livestock or specialize in one breed of horse. They are an outlet for people who want to sell a horse but don't have the time, expertise or interest to sell it on their own. Typically, the horses are a wide range of breeds at a wide range of ages and prices. A good dealer will sell very good, dependable horses.

The Internet

Many horse sites on the Internet have listings of horses for sale, and many dealers have their own websites. This can be a great way to narrow your search; you can even see photos of prospects. This can also give you a sense of what the horse market is like. But ultimately, you should see the horse in person. So again, either limit your search to your area or be prepared to drive some distance to see the horse. You'll want your experienced horse person to come with you, which adds to the complication and expense of looking at long distance.

Professional Trainers

People who educate horses for a living often know of horses that are being sold. Sometimes they have horses for sale themselves that are at their yard for further education, specifically in order for the horse to be more saleable. Making a few calls to trainers may bring up a few prospects. Expect these horses to be on the higher end of your price range, since the seller is not only paying the trainer a commission but also paying for ongoing training and board while the horse is there for sale.

Equine Rescue Shelters

Getting a horse from a rescue shelter can be inexpensive up front, but less experienced people can find themselves with more than they bargained for. Horses often become rescue cases because inexperienced people bring them home and unintentionally let bad habits crop up that then develop into dangerous habits, making the owner afraid to handle the horse. Things get worse when the dangerous habit makes the owner so scared that the horse never gets out of its stable, as that would require someone to handle it. Some owners stop feeding their horses because they are afraid to open the stable door at all. At some point the owner, or perhaps a concerned friend or neighbour, calls equine rescue and the horse is taken away (this is an oversimplification of the process, of course, but this is what often happens).

Often what you are buying at from a dealer is someone else's problem; you often don't get the opportunity to discuss the horse with the owner. Reputable dealers won't sell a beginner a horse that the beginner can't handle, so it's important to learn who is reputable and who is not.

Shelters usually work with the horses first to bring them back to health, and some re-educate the horse in order to increase the odds of a successful placement. If you are experienced enough to carry through the work the shelter has done or to re-educate the horse yourself, getting a horse from a shelter can be an extremely rewarding experience. Some horses simply need a little better handling from the start, and are fine once they are under the care of different people.

Many rescue cases are horses who have chronic health problems and whose owners could no longer afford the care the horses needed or simply lost interest in them because they couldn't ride any more. Navicular disease, arthritis and chronic respiratory problems are just a short list of diseases that can make horses unrideable or able to take only light riding. (As you'll see in Chapter 10, there are some things that you can do to improve chronic problems like this.) It can be very rewarding to give these horses a home as a companion animal to your one riding horse, if you have the time, money and energy to care for them.

Buying From a Distance

Horses are shipped around the country, even around the world, all the time, but a beginner doesn't need to take the time and go to the expense of buying from such a distance. There are lots of good horses within a few hours' drive of your own home. While it can be fun to search the country and look at horses many miles away, you might wait to do that kind of thing until you are a more experienced horse buyer. Why not put the travel money into the horse itself, either to buy a horse further along in its education or to have the horse and/or yourself educated once you get her?

Bring a Trusted Friend

If you are new to horses, the most important thing you can do is bring someone who is experienced with you. This trusted person needs to be someone who knows your skill level and preferably has nothing to gain or lose from the transaction.

The best person to bring with you when looking at horses is simply a knowledgeable friend who has nothing to gain from the purchase except you talking *ad nauseam* about your new horse!

Some people bring their instructor along if they've been taking lessons for a while, or their trainer – the person they plan to work with the horse for them (and, I hope, with the two of you together, too) when they first get it. Just remember that both trainer and instructor have something to gain in the long run; that doesn't make them a bad choice, but their opinions will be based on their own ulterior motives, good or bad, no matter how unbiased they try to be.

Visiting Your Prospects

You've found a horse that fits all your criteria. You've talked to the seller, and everything she told you about the horse makes you even more interested in him. You've arranged a time to come and see the horse. What do you do now?

First, get that friend ready. If you are a beginner rider, bring a friend who would be willing to ride the horse for you. Do whatever it is you need to do – yoga, meditation, drinking hot tea – to calm yourself so that you don't rush into anything. Definitely do not bring a trailer on your first visit! If the horse turns out to be exactly what you want, it helps to be prepared with a deposit, but it may be best to leave your money at home the first time.

Although you'd like to visit your prospect unexpectedly at some point, the first time you go will probably be at a time agreed upon by you and the owner. The owner will probably have the horse all polished up for you, and in a stable or small paddock. She may even have the horse already saddled and waiting. People selling horses spend a lot of time showing them to prospective buyers, so they might want to speed things along a little on your first visit. But during the second visit, when you are much more serious, maybe even ready to put down a deposit if all goes well again, tell the seller you want to see the horse caught and saddled, maybe even asking to catch and saddle the horse yourself.

Although it is a possibility, I doubt there is much in the way of drugging (using tranquillizers or some other substance that temporarily masks the horse's ill behaviour) going on in the horse-selling business. However, there are some mild calming substances or herbal treatments (which a seller is unlikely to tell you about) that can disguise some traits in a horse that might create a little surprise when you get the horse home. Popping in unexpectedly to see the horse can be an educational experience for this reason.

In the excitement of the moment while visiting a horse you might buy, you can forget to ask some important questions. Refer to the checklist overleaf when visiting prospects. Don't put your money down until you have at least learned the answers to the questions listed here!

Watch the seller ride the horse. If the owner/seller is unwilling to ride the horse for you, a beginner might take this as a reason to not buy the horse. A horse that is being sold because it is too much for its seller to ride is not the right horse for a beginner. If the owner has a broken leg (you might ask how that happened), then it is obvious she can't ride the horse for you. But under no circumstances should you – especially if you are not very experienced, and perhaps even if you are – ride the horse before seeing it ridden by someone else, so that you can determine whether your skill level is enough to handle what you see.

General Background

___ How old is the horse?

___ How long have you owned her? Where did you buy her from?

___ Is she registered? (If so, ask to look at her papers. If not, ask what is known about her breeding.)

Riding Experience

___ When was the horse started under saddle? How did that go?

___ Who started her? (If it was a professional trainer, find out his or her name.)

___ What kind of riding has been done with her? Is there a special type of riding that she seems to do the best?

___ Who has ridden her? Beginners? Only experienced riders?

___ What kind of equipment has she been ridden in? (This applies to whether draw reins, particular bits and so on have been used.)

Health History

___ Has she had any health problems? Does she have any chronic illnesses? (If so, ask what you have to do about it.) Does she require any regular medication or special feeding?

___ What does she eat? How many times a day is she fed? Has she ever been out at grass?

___ Has she ever colicked? What was the reason for the colic episode? How was it resolved?

___ What is her shoeing/trimming schedule? Does she require special shoes? Can she go shoeless at any time of year? How is she with the farrier? (Ask whether you can call her farrier and talk with him or her about the horse.)

Handling/Stabling

___ How thorough is the horse's groundwork? Does she accept being tied?

___ Has she been in a trailer? What kind of trailers has she been in? How does she load/unload? How does she travel?

___ What kind of fencing is she accustomed to? Has she ever been around electric fencing?

___ Has she been turned out with other horses? Has she been turned out with other animals, such as sheep, donkeys or goats?

When you have finished looking at the horse and are ready to leave, give the seller a sense of your interest level. Don't commit yourself to anything, but if you are still interested in the horse after the first visit, let the seller know that. Let her know at what stage in your search you are – 'I really like Old Blue, but I've just started looking, so it will be at least a couple of weeks before I get back to you' or 'Old Blue seems pretty close to what I'm looking for, but there are two more on my list, so I want to look at them first'. If you are definitely not interested, say so – 'Old Blue is pretty, but when he bucked you off, I felt nervous'.

If you are interested enough to worry about whether the horse will be sold while you look at your remaining prospects, ask if you can have first refusal on the horse. If someone else comes along who's interested, the seller will call and let you know that you need to make a decision. Many sellers may not be willing to do this, but it's worth a try, especially if you have looked at quite a few horses and Old Blue comes the closest yet to what you want.

The Vetting Exam

You've decided on a horse that meets your needs and appeals to you enough to make you want to bring it home and tend to it two or three times a day, seven days a week, 365 days a year. Whether you want the horse checked over by a vet before you finalize the sale is up to you – the seller probably won't suggest it.

Veterinary examinations are very common – rather like a home inspection before buying a house – and all large animal veterinary practices have a standard exam they administer. If the seller won't allow a vetting to take place, walk away from the sale. With horses, it is definitely a 'let the buyer beware' situation. If it's your choice not to have the horse checked by a vet, fine, but you need to know that you are taking a chance.

Don't forget to do the following things with each of your prospects:
- Watch the horse being tacked up and ridden by someone else.
- Tack and ride the horse yourself.
- After the first visit, visit the stable unannounced to see your prospective purchase.
- Look at the horse's registration papers, if there are any.
- Get a veterinarian to do a vetting exam.
- If you have any serious reservations, don't buy the horse.

In a vetting exam, the vet checks the horse's temperature, heart rate and other vital signs, and also performs some general lameness and range of motion tests. You may decide to have other tests done as well – these may need to be arranged separately, and will usually cost extra. For instance, if you are buying the horse with a specific performance activity in mind, such as jumping, you may want the doctor to X-ray leg joints, specifically knees and feet. If you are going to use a mare for breeding, ask the vet to look specifically at the horse's reproductive system.

If you are looking for a performance horse, even if you are at the beginner level, you will definitely want to have it vetted. The basic exam takes around 90 minutes, and both you and the seller should be there. It can be done at the seller's facility, or the horse can be transported to a veterinary facility. Either way, the potential buyer typically pays for the exam and everything related to it.

The exam is an assessment tool, not a pass-or-fail test. Here are the most important items to be informed about:

· Does the horse have a chronic illness or injury that isn't obvious to you, the layperson?
· If the horse has a known injury or illness, how severe is it and will it interfere with what you want to do with the horse? There may be some things that come up that don't have any impact on how you plan to use

the horse and, therefore, don't count as a reason to walk away. But keep in mind that if you decide to sell the horse in the future, a chronic injury or illness may make the pool of potential buyers smaller and the horse harder to sell.

- Does anything about the horse's conformation make her unable or unlikely to be able to do what you plan to ask of her? For instance, an underbite in the horse's teeth has nothing to do with her ability to jump; it can, however, decrease her ability to efficiently digest her food and, therefore, make it difficult for her to maintain weight, ultimately lessening her energy and stamina for jumping. The underbite may not be a reason not to buy the horse if everything else about her is what you want – age, size, colour, temperament, price – but you should find out whether the horse will require any special tooth work or feeding, either now or as she ages.

The veterinarian will share the results of the examination with you and the seller, and will provide you with a written copy. While the veterinarian is there, bring up any health questions you may have about the horse that are not covered in the general exam.

The Big Purchase

You've viewed your prospect being ridden, ridden him yourself more than once (unless you're buying an unstarted horse), handled the horse and perhaps brushed him and led him around the yard. You can't stop thinking about him and talking about him. He's been checked over by a veterinarian and given a clean bill of health. You're ready to buy.

When you inform the seller of your decision, you will probably be required to give a good-sized deposit to hold the horse. When you are ready to take him to his next home, you will need to pay the balance in full, unless you have made other arrangements with the seller.

Getting Your Horse Home

Arranging transportation shouldn't be too difficult; the sellers may be able to deliver him to you for a fee, or perhaps you have an experienced horse friend with a trailer. (This is where it will help to know about the horse's travelling history, both loading and riding, and what kind of trailer he's accustomed to.)

If you are not yet ready to take your horse to his final destination, the seller may be able to keep him for you for a short period of time; it depends on the situation. For example, a seller with a livery yard may be happy to have him stay on as long as you pay, but a trainer may need to get him out as soon as possible to open up a stable for a new student.

Registration Transfer

If he is a registered animal, there will be a transfer of registration papers. The breed associations all operate a little differently, but in general the current owner will send in the transfer information and then the breed registry will send the new papers to you with your name added to them. Alternatively, the owner (who may or may not be the seller) can sign the papers over to you, and then you send them to the breed registry. Transferring registration is usually not very expensive. However, you should get this done immediately, as this is an important part of the monetary value of your horse. If the horse is not registered, a simple bill of sale, including a description of the horse, should suffice.

When you buy your horse, you will need to change the owner details in its passport. This involves returning the passport to the issuing organization. Passports are a record of a horse's appearance and any veterinary treatment it has received, but they don't prove that the passport holder is the owner of the horse.

A Smooth Transition

Finally, find out what your horse eats; this is something you should ask when you are still looking at him. What the horse eats can tell you a bit about his temperament and how easy he is to keep. Make sure you stock up on the same brand and type of food before your horse comes home. Eventually, you will develop your own likes and dislikes when it comes to brands and types of feed, but for now you should feed him what he's been accustomed to.

If there are other horses in the yard in which he is going to live and you plan to change your new horse to what the others eat, ask the seller for a five- to six-day supply of the food he's currently eating in order to switch him over gradually. Alternatively, buy a bag and plan to switch him over the course of that bag of feed. (See Chapter 7 for suggestions on switching food.)

Have a place prepared for him: a safe stable or shelter with fresh bedding, with a place for a water bucket and a feed tub, a mineral block, a supply of hay, a wheelbarrow and manure fork, and a solidly fenced turnout area are the least you'll need for your own set-up. Even if you are keeping your new horse at livery, you'll need a halter and a lead rope and a few grooming supplies; for example, brushes and a hoof pick.

When you get your new horse to where he is going to live, let him settle in for a few days and get to know you and his new environment. If there are other horses there, he is probably going to be a lot more interested in them than in you. Don't throw a saddle on him the minute you get him out of the trailer. Spend some time with him, groom him and allow him to settle down a little. Some horses adapt very easily and will settle easily into a stable with a section of hay and happily munch and look around. Others are more easily unsettled and will be restless for a while, their senses on high alert, pacing their stable, and stopping to listen to every noise and look at every movement. Give the horse – and his new owner! – some time to settle into the place it is hoped he will call home.

Loaning or Leasing

There is a way to acquire a horse without actually owning it, and that is through loaning or leasing. Sometimes the current life circumstances of a horse's owner – pregnancy, health problems, temporary relocation for a job, a new job that takes up more time – make it impossible for the owner to give the horse the attention it needs. Usually loans are 'free' (in that they do not have a monthly rental fee attached to them), but, like everything else, there are a number of ways it can be done.

Why Loan?

One very logical reason to loan a horse is so that you can 'trade up' as your skills advance, especially if you compete. Imagine, for instance, that you plan to learn dressage. If you spend the time and energy to get to the top levels of dressage competition, you will probably go through three or four horses on your way there. The horse who is laid back enough to be a beginner dressage horse may not have what it takes to be the Grand Prix candidate you want when your own skill level gets that advanced. If you have the space, you can collect these horses as you progress up the ranks; more probably, you will need to sell them and put the money towards your next prospect. However, if you loan the horse, you can simply give it back to the owner when you are ready to move on.

The Loan Agreement

A loan may have a stipulation that the horse needs to remain at either the owner's house or at the yard where the horse is being kept. This is probably your biggest consideration after whether your skill level matches the education of the horse. Make sure you sign a loan agreement, or at least a letter of agreement, outlining the following details of the arrangement, plus anything else that you can think of:

· Who pays for maintenance items such as shoes and vaccinations?
· Is there an end date? Leaving the loan open-ended is probably not a good idea; it is better to make the loan easy to renew by inserting a phrase that allows it to continue for the same period of time (one year seems logical) simply by having both parties sign new signatures on the existing agreement.

- Where can the horse be kept? What kind of shelter is sufficient? You may think a field shelter with 24/7 turnout is perfect, but the owner may expect the horse to be in a box at night.
- Can the horse be turned out with other horses?
- Are you allowed to trailer the horse to a horse show, pleasure ride or whatever? Can the horse be taken far afield? And kept overnight?
- What happens if the horse needs emergency veterinary care? Who makes decisions about that care, and who pays for it?
- What happens if the horse dies while it is under your care? Of course, no one wants this to happen, but it could.

However the actual loan agreement is set up, proceed with your decision-making process as if you were buying the horse – that is, watch the owner or someone else ride the horse, handle it, ride it yourself and so on. If this is the route you want to go down, your selection will be slimmer. However, since you are not going to own the horse, you may be willing to overlook some things. Many loans end up with the borrower purchasing the horse, so bear that in mind too. Some people don't like to loan because they are worried about getting too attached to the horse and having a hard time giving it up when the agreement comes to an end.

If you are a parent buying your child's first horse, follow all of the same advice given in this chapter. Don't mount your child on a horse beyond his or her abilities – even the most gentle horse is still a large and unintentionally dangerous animal.

Last, there are also 'shared loans', in which you share a horse, often at a riding stable, with someone else. You each are assigned specific days, or even times, that you can ride the horse. Typically, the stable is responsible for all the horse's care but uses sharing to cover a portion of its upkeep. This is a reasonable way for stables that keep a string of riding horses to ensure that each horse pays its own way. Be sure to arrange sharing with a responsible riding school, however; you don't want to find out that your mount is being shared between four people, used for lessons and ridden five times a day, seven days a week. In addition, make sure that there are not so many different people riding the horse that there is never any consistency in handling. Horses can develop some very bad habits from this kind of use; if this is the case, make sure that the horse's bad habits are ones you can deal with.

Congratulations!

Soon you will realize your dream and have your own horse! Whatever you lack in experience now, be assured that as the years go by you will look back and amaze yourself at how much experience you have gained. Taking care of a horse of your own will seem as natural a part of your daily routine as brushing your teeth.

CHAPTER 6

Stabling

Between this chapter and the last, you became the caretaker of a horse. Now you need to keep her somewhere. You basically have three options: a livery yard; your own yard; or the yard of a friend, acquaintance or neighbour. Each one of these options has its complications and its benefits.

Choosing a Livery Yard

The basic premise of keeping a horse at livery is simple: you pay money to someone who has gone to the expense of constructing stables that hold many horses, and that person more or less takes full care of housing and feeding your horse and of the everyday maintenance of the facility, including mucking out your horse's stable. Simple? It can be. However, it can also be extremely complicated.

Daily stable cleaning is important. Start by picking out the large piles, then sifting around the bedding for the scattered chunks, and then moving away the top part of the bedding and digging out the wet spots. About once a week (maybe more if your horse is in its stable for long periods of time), strip stables of all bedding and let the stable air out for as long as possible. Sprinkle lime or stable cleaner on the wet spots to reduce odours before putting down fresh bedding.

You do have several decisions to make when it comes to keeping your horse at livery. Let's take a closer look at some of them.

Location

Your first consideration is probably going to be the proximity of the livery yard to your home or perhaps to your job. I used to keep my mare at a yard halfway between work and home. On the weekends, I didn't mind the drive, and during the week, I could stop by on my way home from work to ride, groom or simply check her. It is a good idea to first look for places near either home or work to make it easier for you to spend the most time with your horse.

Stabling

If you are a first-time horse owner, you may not have much of an opinion about how your horse is stabled. But you will develop your own preferences in time. If your ideas change from what is offered at your current yard, you can always move your horse.

Yards offer different arrangements, but the most likely scenario is that your horse will have a stable in which he will spend a good deal of time. The larger the stable the better – a minimum of 4 x 4m (12 x 12ft) is preferable, and larger is even better, but then you'll use huge amounts of bedding. (Any yard trying to make a living probably won't want to spend the extra time and money on oversized stables – larger stables means fewer stables, and that means fewer liveries).

Ex-champion jockey and award-winning author Dick Francis published his first novel, *Dead Cert*, in 1962. Close to 40 mystery novels later, he has made a successful living. With the racing industry as the backdrop, his worldwide bestsellers have been translated into over 30 languages. Easy to get hooked on, Francis's novels include such titles as *Field of Thirteen*, *Bolt*, *Wild Horses*, *High Stakes* and *Blood Sport*.

The best arrangement for a horse is a field shelter with 24-hour turnout (see the following section for more on turnout), but facilities offering this all year round are few and far between. It is mostly about convenience – it is much easier to feed horses and clean stables that are all in one place than it is to trudge through the weather to outside shelters. A few enlightened yards with many stables under one roof are set up so that there are small turnout areas outside each stable, essentially for the horse to have a stretch outside when he wants. This, along with turnout in a larger area during the day when you aren't exercising your horse, can be the best of all. With this arrangement, your horse is near the tack room and riding arena, if there is one, but still gets 24/7 turnout, albeit in a small area for part of the time.

Horses seem to be more content when they have at least some control over their situation – for example, being in the sun or in the shade, out in the snow or in a cozy stable with deep bedding.

Turnout

Facilities differ greatly in what they offer for turnout for each horse. You should know how many hours a day each horse gets out. In ads for livery yards, you might read 'half-day turnout', which means that each horse gets approximately four hours of the day out of its stable – which is perhaps OK if you ride every day, but not nearly enough if you don't! Are the horses all turned out in a big pasture ('pasture turnout') after feeding in the morning, and do they spend the day there until they are brought in for evening feeding and for the night? Do they get just two hours each by themselves in a collection of small paddocks? The more time your horse is out of its stable, the better. Is it important to you whether or not your horse gets turned out with other horses? You will need to make that clear to the yard manager.

What does turnout mean?
Turnout refers to the period when your horse is out of the confinement of her stable and loose in a larger area – either outside in a paddock, or in an indoor arena if the weather is bad.

Facilities

Is there a riding arena? If you live somewhere where ice and snow are a concern during the winter months, and/or work nine to five, you'll probably want to keep your horse where there is an indoor arena. If there is no indoor arena, does the outdoor arena have lights? Is it OK to use them? How early in the morning or how late in the evening is it OK for you to come and use the facilities?

Find out how many liveries the yard takes on. Are the riding areas big enough for the number of horses? Is there good hacking nearby? (See 'Keeping Your Horse at Home' later in this chapter for other things to consider at livery yards, such as what to look for in stable floors.)

Type of Riding

The livery yards I have enjoyed the most have been those that have an eclectic group of riders of all different types of riding disciplines and from competitive riders to plain hackers. But if you are interested in learning about a particular type of riding, you might want to find a yard that concentrates on one particular kind of riding so that you can really expand your knowledge in that area. A yard that specializes in jumping will probably have a nice cross-country course, some good low-level training jumps in the arena, will perhaps include members of the local hunt , and may hold jumping clinics that you can participate in without having to travel.

The Livery Agreement

It is a good idea to ask to see the livery agreement that you will be expected to sign if you bring your horse to stay at the yard. You should note anything that you are expected to supply or do; also note when rent is due and what happens if you are late with payment. Try to think of anything that you may have forgotten to ask about, such as whether there are specific times when you can use the facilities; whether there are any other requirements, such as wearing a riding helmet; or whether there are any limitations on the number of riders allowed at a time in the arena, and so on.

Read the agreement very carefully. If there is anything you do not understand, ask for an explanation. If there is anything you are uncomfortable with, don't hesitate to ask whether that particular point in the contract can be altered – you never know unless you ask! Don't feel trapped into signing an agreement that you are uncomfortable with – go somewhere else.

Other Owners

Before signing on the dotted line, you should spend some time at the yard, meeting some of the other owners and watching them work with their horses. Ask them whether they like being there. Owners come and go pretty regularly for all sorts of reasons (but if there is a huge turnover, you might want to find out why), so if there's one person whose style you don't appreciate – maybe she's got a quick temper with her horse, or maybe he seems to take over the indoor arena when he's riding – it probably isn't a reason not to keep your horse there.

But if everyone seems to work their horses hard and then put them away dripping with sweat, or if people argue with each other about how to use the arena, then maybe the general atmosphere doesn't suit you. It's hard to know everything in a couple of hours, but you should be able to sense any major problems. What you will most probably find is a congenial group of horse enthusiasts who welcome a new horse and rider into their fold.

Cost

Expect the cost to vary widely from yard to yard, depending on the location and facilities on offer. The closer you get to more populated areas, the more livery is likely to cost. A 30-acre yard in a highly desirable area with limited open land left, where developers are drooling over the houses they could build and sell on the land, means that the yard almost certainly cost a lot to construct, and the monthly rental charges will reflect that.

Services will cost you as well. Some yards include riding lessons. Some offer such things as holding your horse for the farrier or vet, or rugging when necessary. Some places offer worming programmes to keep all horses on the same schedule. Expect a higher cost for more amenities – such as a wash room for horses, a tack shop on the premises, a nice tack storage area with personal lockers, a heated lounge area, food to purchase on the premises, toilets and showers, and maybe even a vet or farrier on the premises of larger yards. There is a cost associated with the owner to provide these things, and in order for the yard to stay in business, the cost must be passed along to the liveries.

Other Details

Here are some other things to consider and ask about:

- Does the stable practise good safety habits? Look for a neatly kept yard with things such as water hoses coiled up and out of the way of horses and people. Access areas should be clear of debris and not used for storage. Feed should be stored in an area separate from the horse stables, behind a latched gate or door, and neatly kept in rodent-proof storage bins. Although you can't expect to eat off the floors, a good sweeping of the common areas once a day, and perhaps evidence of an annual cleaning of the dust generated from horses coming and going, shows a commitment to quality in other areas as well. Also, find out whether the driveways are clear of rubbish and quickly cleared of snow in the winter.

· Are the stables constructed safely and without protrusions that could injure your horse? Look for feeders for hay and coarse mix that are appropriate for horses – they certainly don't have to be fancy, but they should be without sharp edges or holes. Are the stables pretty clean on your visits? Stable doors should open and close with ease and bolt easily. It's nice when name cards are put on each stable door telling who the horse is, what she eats, any peculiarities such as allergies or unusual habits (such as the ability to unlatch a stable door), and how to contact her owner in case of emergency.

· Are there good fire prevention measures, such as 'no smoking' signs, fire extinguishers and up-to-date electrical wiring? Is there an evacuation plan in the event of fire? Many stables offer owners the choice of having a halter left on their horse in the stable for quicker evacuation in case of fire, or leaving the halter hanging on the door. Does anyone perform a night check, which can be as simple as a walk through the yard, looking in each stable? Does the night check include an evening snack for everyone, or a topping up of water buckets? If it is a large yard that houses many horses and has lots of people milling around all the time, you might want to make sure that there is someone on the premises at most times, and that the stable can be seen from the home of the owner or manager.

· Is there good security for your horse and your tack? You should be comfortable leaving your saddle there; otherwise, you'll have to carry it back and forth from your car. If there is trailer parking space available, you could leave some things in your trailer, especially if you have a locking tack area. Find out whether other owners are respectful of your things; they should not use them without permission (except in the case of an emergency, of course).

- Do the horses get ample water in their stables and out in the paddocks/pastures? The stable should have a good plan for providing ice-free water in the winter. Look for clean water buckets and containers that are large enough for the number of horses turned out in one area.
- Are there places in the pasture for horses to get away from flies or cold wind? A nice hedgerow will block the wind during the coldest times of the year if it is placed in the right spot (see Chapter 7 for a list of some common poisonous shrubs to watch out for). In the peak of fly season, horses need either a place to escape to or plenty of attention with fly sprays, sheets and masks. Is the pasture shelter big enough for the number of horses turned out there? Typically, one horse can guard a surprisingly large area, leaving no space for any other horse. Horses can be switched around so that those that don't compete so much with each other can share.
- Will the yard add supplements to your horse's feed at your request (and expense, of course)? Some stables charge extra per supplement per day; 24 horses that require an average of two supplements each added to their feed twice a day can add up to a lot of extra time for caretakers, so it's hard to blame them!
- What about those times when your horse needs medical attention? Can you pay someone to fill in for you if the horse needs to be walked three times a day for a week or have a bandage changed if you can't make it every day?

Keeping Your Horse With a Friend or Neighbour

Another viable and common option is to keep a horse with a friend who already has a horse or two. Usually the financial arrangements work well for both of you. Your friend will probably charge you a lot less than the going rate at the local livery yard, since she is not in business; with luck, she might charge just enough for her time and to cover the feed costs for her own horse(s).

Your friend might be the one doing all the work, since she will want to clean stables and such according to her own schedule and standard of care, but there are many different arrangements you can make. If your friend is close enough to your home, you could share feeding responsibilities; for example, one of you does it in the morning and the other at night. In exchange for fairly cheap board, you could provide all your own feed and muck out your own stable, but of course the owner of the yard will have the final say in how the arrangement is set up.

Dogs and horses don't always mix. Some dogs love to chase horses. If the pursuit is hot enough, they can chase them right through fences, causing all sorts of damage. And your dog can get hurt as well. So teach your dogs early on that horses are off-limits.

Advantages

There are several advantages to keeping your horse at a friend's house. For one thing, you have a built-in riding partner. In addition, during the hay-making season, you can chip in and help each other bring in the year's supply. If you are new to horse-keeping, you have someone to help you as you learn about caring for a horse.

Disadvantages

However, there are also some disadvantages:

·   If this person has been a friend for a while, you could run into a disagreement that could end your friendship. The best thing to help avoid that is to try to be upfront about everything and cover all the possible problems before you bring your horse to her house.
·   If the person was not a friend in the past, you may find you simply don't get along. If that happens, find a new place to keep your horse and move him as soon as possible. People who aren't fond of the owner of the yard are often less inclined to visit their horses.
·   In a setting that is more private than a livery yard, you may sometimes feel as if you are intruding when you want to see your horse. For

example, if the owner has family visiting and there's a football game going in the garden, you might feel uncomfortable being there.

· You may not get a lot of the perks that a livery yard offers, such as access to a toilet, a riding arena and some of the anonymity that comes with the larger facility.

It all depends on the situation. Many people have several stables at their private home and can easily board the horses of friends or neighbours. When the yard is a bit away from the house and has a rustic loo, the situation can work out very well.

Take advantage of opportunities. For example, if your friend goes to ballet practice with her daughter on Monday and Thursday nights, pick those evenings to spend some time at the yard on your own. If the situation works most of the time, find ways to work around the small problems.

Keeping Your Horse at Home

Perhaps you have planned all along to keep your horse at your own home. This is the best arrangement of all – you get to decide everything about how your horse lives and to do things your own way, and you get to spend the maximum amount of time with your horse – if you have only 15 minutes and can't fit in a ride, you can groom your horse without having to travel to do it.

Of course, when you keep your horse at home, you will also be doing all the day-to-day maintenance. This is a serious matter to think about ahead of time. Do you have the time to clean stables, make trips to the feed store, hold your horse for the farrier, install and mend fences and so on? If you were travelling for 20–30 minutes to the livery yard, perhaps you do have the time – that one-hour round trip could have been used to do some maintenance tasks. But remember that you travel to the livery yard only *if you want to*. If your horse is in your back garden, you can't miss feeding him for a day or two because you either don't have the time or don't feel like it.

Is it Allowed?

Just because you have a big garden, it doesn't follow that you can keep your horse in it. If you have a small paddock or field that hasn't been used as a home for livestock for a long time, it is best to check with the local authority that you are allowed to keep your horse there, especially if you live in a built-up area.

Give 'em Shelter

If you plan to build stables, your options are limited only by the amount of space you have, your budget and planning regulations. If you have a minimal amount of space, plan to have just one or two horses, and would like to leave most of the space for your horse(s) to run around in, consider a field shelter. Horses can live perfectly well in this situation, even in the most severe weather. If you expect two horses to use the shelter, it will have to be big enough for two horses to share, which can mean more space than you might think! Ideally, the shelter should have a standard stable space for each horse that will use it – that is, two horses should have a shelter that is 4 x 8m (12 x 24ft), or a 4 x 4m (12 x 12ft) stable space per horse. The nice thing about this set-up is that you could put a temporary panel down the middle and create two stables with turnout areas for night-time or emergencies.

The main problem with having just a field shelter is the fact that you will have to make separate arrangements to store feed and tack, and grooming and tacking up can be difficult, unless the shelter is near your storage area and you can arrange tie-up points in it. Although a garden shed will be adequate for feed and tack, hay or other forage is a different matter. Unless you are prepared to keep going to the supplier every few days, you will need to find somewhere to store enough for a month or so.

FIGURE 6.1:
Field shelter

Field shelters are comparatively simple to construct, and you can often buy them prefabricated from mail-order catalogues, horse building specialists and local farm suppliers or timber merchants. Most of these will be adaptable to your situation and the size you need. Alternatively, you could ask a local carpenter to build one for you, and this gives you the chance to customize it somewhat.

If you want to build stables, your first hurdle will be getting planning permission. This is often relatively easy if you simply want to erect a wooden building, but if you want something more permanent, you may find it difficult to get the planners to agree. You will need to get plans drawn up – or do some research and draw them yourself – and find a builder or carpenter who can make the building safe for horses. Make sure you consider every last item, such as ensuring that the light switches are waterproof and away from the stabling, that water supplies are adequate, that the doors into the stables are wide enough and that the stables will face away from the prevailing weather.

There are always things to repair or replace when you keep horses. Plan to have at least one extra water bucket, feed tub and so on around to replace broken ones without having to make a special trip to the supply store. If something is wearing out, replace or mend it before it gives out. The more you keep up with things, the more you are in control – and the more free time you have for riding.

Using an Existing Structure

Maybe your property already has some stables that have been used for horses in the past. If so, this can make your job a little easier. If horses were there fairly recently, the stables are likely to be in pretty good shape – but everyone has different standards for housing horses, so you'll want to check it out thoroughly to see if the building meets yours. If it was used for a different purpose or even a different kind of animal, the first thing you need to do is examine it closely inside and out, looking for anything that might have been OK for a goat but that spells trouble for a horse. If you are new to horses, get a knowledgeable friend to look over it with you.

Get rid of protruding nails, replace or cover glass windows that will be within reach of the horse (or a horse's flying hooves!) at any time, and look for anything that might cause a horse's hoof to get caught. Are there any electric cables within reach of the horse's stable, or old rusted chicken wire, for example? Move it or block the horse's access to it. Make sure that stable doors and the like are high enough to contain a horse, and ensure that stable doors and exterior doors open wide enough to get a horse in and out without the horse constantly hitting his hip on the door frame.

Do not underestimate the strength of a horse! When building walls, hanging gates, creating fencing or constructing anything that is to contain a horse, consider situations such as the horse putting all its weight on the wall to scratch its hind end. Anything you build needs to be strong enough to take this kind of treatment from a half-ton animal.

Another thing you should consider is the orientation of the building. The stables I have created in a former cow barn are pretty open and have nice southern exposure. However, if your horse is in its stable a lot, you won't want it to bake in the sun all day and will want to be sure the horse has a shady area to retire to.

Flooring

There are two main types of stable flooring: concrete and earth.

Concrete

Concrete is the most common form of stable flooring by far. Concrete floors are hard on a horse's legs, as they don't offer any give. If this is what you've got, covering the floor with rubber mats and a deep layer of bedding to cushion your horse's legs will help. Rubber mats will also help if the concrete is smooth and potentially slippery. On the other hand, concrete does have two advantages: it holds up to hard wear extremely well, and it can be hosed down.

Earth

Earth floors are quite rare but are the best – there are no issues of being sturdy enough, they are fine for horses' legs, and, depending on the type of earth, the urine doesn't settle on the surface for the horses to lounge around in. However, the urine does sink in, and earth floors therefore retain the smell of urine and don't have the advantage of being able to be hosed down.

If the earth floor does not get a lot of exposure to the sun, you will need to be extra diligent in cleaning out wet spots daily and perhaps do a full muck out more frequently than required with other types of stable flooring. Whenever you muck out and put down clean bedding, you can help reduce the odour problem by spreading some lime or other odour-reducing products on the urine spots beforehand. And don't forget that urine odour is not just unpleasant; the fumes are bad for your horse's respiratory health.

Different Kinds of Bedding

Like everything to do with horses, you will soon decide that you prefer one type of bedding over the others. Basically, the choices are shavings (or sawdust) or straw. Other options include hemp waste and shredded paper. The advantages of shavings are that they usually come in convenient, easily stored, plastic-wrapped bales and they are easy to use – you use a muck fork to remove the muck, and the shavings fall back into the bed. They are low in dust, so are suitable for horses with respiratory problems. Hay is cheaper, but comes in large bales and is not that good for horses with respiratory problems. Rubber mats are becoming more popular, but generally need hay or shavings on top to soak up urine and around the edge to prevent the horse getting cast.

If you are putting a horse into a field with stock fencing or a hedge or bank, check that it is safe and secure all the way around. For a stock fence to be suitable for horses it must have mesh that is too small for a hoof to go through. While it is possible to keep a horse safely in other conditions, it is rarely worth the risk.

Fencing

Don't bring your horse home until you have your fences up. Fencing is critical. For horses, electric fencing and post and rails are often best, but you will probably find that you end up with a mixture of post and rails, electric fencing, stock fencing, hedges, banks and walls, depending on where you live. Whatever you do, don't put a horse into a field with barbed wire – it just isn't worth it. Also, don't use only electric fencing – it is far too easy for a horse to break through it and get out onto the road.

Electric Fencing
Electric fencing is probably the most commonly used for horses in the yard set-up. It is inexpensive, easily installed by even an amateur, and

easily moved and reconfigured. To use electric fencing successfully, three essential ingredients are required:

1. **Fence posts:** These can be metal or plastic, and they come with built-in insulators.
2. **Fence wire:** There are quite a few different kinds of electric fence wire. The more common types are flat tape, smooth wire and rope.
3. **A fence charger:** Basically, electric- or battery-operated fence chargers are your choices. Make sure the charger is grounded properly so that if either the wire or the charger gets hit by a lightning bolt, it will run into the ground.

Post and Rails

Post-and-rail fencing is beautiful, but expensive. People who use it often also add electric wire to keep the horses from chewing it, so it becomes double fencing.

Water

As discussed in Chapter 7, your horse will need access to fresh water, day in and day out, every season of the year. If you don't have an automatic trough, fill a large container once or twice a day, depending on how many horses you have, and their sizes.

Carrying heavy water buckets can cause back and neck problems, but lifting and carrying heavy things is a fact of life for horse owners. Learn good body mechanics and how to lift by using your knees to avoid putting a strain on your back.

If you live in an area that regularly goes below freezing in the winter, getting water to your horse can be a chore. The best solution is to bring the horse a bucket of fresh 'warm' water at each feeding time, and to leave a bucket in a sheltered site during the day.

Feed Storage

Store your horse's feed in a place that is not easily accessible to the horse if she happens to get loose. Coarse mix and other hard feeds take up little space – a dustbin in the corner of the garage can work well, with perhaps a shelf next to it for a container of supplements, a scoop or other paraphernalia. Hay also needs good storage space, free from dust and dampness, and definitely not open to the weather. With a horse eating half a bale or more a day when stabled, you should aim to store 15–20 bales if possible.

Manure

Don't forget to think about manure management before your horse walks onto the property! Your horse will start generating it immediately, and the supply will be constant.

There may be a gardener nearby who would just love to take your manure away on a regular basis. Alternatively, if you can pile it in an accessible place, you can put a sign out by the road and allow people to help themselves. Of course, if you have your own garden, you may not want to give it away, but bear in mind that there's a never-ending supply!

Tack/Equipment Storage

You will need some storage for your tack and other equipment. If you have an existing building, consider where you could make some space in which to keep your tack. Make sure that it is no great distance from the area where you will tack up your horse – you don't want to have to carry your saddle 100 metres every time you ride, or stand in the rain or cold wind next to your garden shed to tack up.

Other pieces of equipment to be stored include a wheelbarrow and manure fork, turnout rugs and grooming supplies. These items do not take up an extraordinary amount of space, but you will be amazed at how quickly you begin to collect equine paraphernalia!

The Law

Now is as good a time as any to talk about some legal issues concerning horses. Ask people on the street to describe something about horses; right after 'they're beautiful', they will probably bring up 'dangerous', 'strong' or 'flighty'. It's true that, if for no other reason than their sheer size and weight compared to humans, horses are inherently dangerous. Combine that with a decision-making process and reasoning largely unknown to us, and you have a potential recipe for disaster.

Many of us take that risk willingly. But being hurt – stepped on, kicked, bucked off – is always possible.

If you allow someone else to ride your horse, even on a very casual basis, check that they are insured for personal liability. Children under 18, or even over 18 but still living at home, may be covered under their parents' household policy; otherwise, some horse insurance companies will offer rider-only policies. Whatever you do, don't simply trust that an accident will never happen!

Your Responsibility

If you own a horse, get insurance for personal liability. Put simply, this means that you must make sure that you are covered if your horse causes damage to someone or their property. The simple fact of being a horse owner means that you will be responsible if it escapes from the field or kicks a car, or anything else in that line. Although large claims will usually go to court and the insurance companies will battle it out, you still need to be insured. At the moment, most household insurance policies will cover you to a certain extent, because horses are not excluded on them, but this may change as claims increase in our ever more litigious society. Your horse insurance should cover you, too.

If you become a Gold Member of the British Horse Society, you can get free legal advice. You will also have cover for personal liability and personal accident – although it is best to have other insurance policies as well.

Decisions Aren't Always Final

Make your decisions about where to keep your horse using the same key decision-making process as you do for everything else that is important. Keep in mind that livery decisions can be changed, but if you don't feel happy about a situation before you go into it, save yourself some headaches and don't do it.

If you are going to keep your horse at home, it is important to have the basics in place before you bring your horse back there. But remember, you will develop your likes and dislikes about things like fencing, feed and even the types of buckets you use as you get experience, so don't buy everything at once. And keep in mind that things can be changed!

CHAPTER 7

Nutrition

Feeding your horse can be a delicate task. As you discovered in Chapter 3, the horse's digestive system is an amazing yet poorly constructed vehicle for processing the amounts of food needed by this large animal.

To cut to the basics, most domestic horses need grass, grain, hay and water to provide the essentials that their bodies need – water, energy, protein, carbohydrates, fatty acids, minerals and vitamins. But each of those areas of horse nutrition has branches galore; if you mix in supplements, you can quickly need a computer program to work it all out. Keep the feeding of your horse as simple as you can, while taking the individual needs of your horse into consideration.

First, There is Water

Clean, potable water provided in clean containers day and night during spring, summer, autumn and winter, is critical to the health and well-being of your horse. Without it, food cannot make its journey through the system, nutrients cannot be transported to and through the bloodstream, body temperature cannot be regulated, and waste and toxins cannot be eliminated. Without a steady supply of water, horses risk colic from food sitting in their digestive tract and fermenting or packing up and preventing the passage of manure. Water is vital.

According to James M. Griffin and Tom Gore in the *Horse Owner's Veterinary Handbook*: 'When deprived of water for two days, a horse generally refuses to eat and may show signs of colic. With ideal weather and good health, a horse might be able to live for five or six days without water.'

How Much?

The average horse of around 450kg (1,000lb) drinks around 38l (8gal) of water per day. That amount goes up or down according to the size of the horse. But it also increases if the horse works more than an hour or so a day, or if a mare is feeding her foal. If temperatures are extreme in either direction, hot or cold, the horse will require more water to replenish lost fluids and keep his interior temperature constant. Keeping fresh water available to the horse at all times allows him to choose how much water he needs. At first, you might find you are wasting water. The longer you take care of your horse, the more you will realize how much is too much while still giving your horse a free choice.

Providing Water

Unfortunately, providing horses with fresh water can sometimes be a pain. In spring, summer and autumn, it's fairly simple – either rely on automatic fillers or use a hose. In winter , you might have problems with freezing, which means trekking to and fro with buckets from the house.

make sure to lag outside taps, and keep a kettle in your tack room for really cold mornings.

Do whatever you need to do, and use whatever you are most comfortable with to keep fresh water in front of your horse. It is critical that horses drink, especially in cold weather.

Keep Buckets Clean

Plan to clean your water buckets regularly. If the buckets sit where they are exposed to the sun, algae and scum form quickly. Make bucket cleaning an easy task so that you won't mind doing it. Choose a bucket and water tub cleaning tool – a rag, a washing sponge, a brush made just for bucket washing, a toilet bowl brush and so on – and keep it handy (but out of reach of the horses). Once a week or so, round up all the buckets (include feed buckets), give them a good washing and let them dry in bacteria-killing sunshine.

Forage

Apart from grass, hay or other forage, such as haylage, is the horse's most important foodstuff. The digestion of forage keeps the horse warm in winter, from the inside out, and provides the roughage to keep the digestive process moving along.

Forage can get complicated. It involves finding a source, determining what type you want, working out how much to get and making sure that the supply you get is good quality.

If you keep your horse at livery, of course, you don't need to worry about most of this. However, you should be sure that your livery stable does. When investigating facilities, don't be shy about asking to see their forage, what kind it is and where their supply comes from. Even if you don't know the best answers yourself, a good facility will consider these things important and know the answers to those questions about their own forage.

Haylage is fast becoming as popular as hay with horse owners. It is baled slightly earlier than hay and wrapped in plastic so that it stays moist and ferments slightly. This means that its nutritional content is higher than hay and, because it is moist, it is ideal for feeding to horses that are sensitive to the mould spores in hay.

Finding a Supplier

One of the nice things about having livestock such as horses is that it puts you in touch with the agricultural community. Finding and keeping a good hay or haylage supply will introduce you to local farmers. Before you bring your new horse home, look for a supplier and buy a decent amount, depending on how much storage space you have. You should plan to keep at least a month's supply plus a few extra bales in case you run late when getting your next month's supply.

Ask other local horse owners where they get their forage – farmers like good customers who pass their names along. On the other hand, if it was a bad year and supplies are low, horse owners can be reluctant to pass along their source!

It's important to change hard feed gradually over a period of a few days. It's also good to introduce your horse gradually to the new season's crop of freshly cut forage. Make sure you have a few bales left from last year's supply when the new supply comes. If you don't have any older forage left to mix in with the new, take extra time over a few days to feed the new forage in smaller quantities and give your horse more frequent meals spread out across the day.

The Agricultural Store

The agricultural store is certainly a place to ask about local farmers, and most stores usually carry baled hay and haylage. This is often high in quality, but the supply can be unreliable and it is probably going to be one of the most expensive ways to buy forage. If you have only one horse, this may be an ideal source for you – you can get hay or haylage, shavings, feed, supplements and any other supplies all in one monthly or twice-monthly shopping trip, and the additional cost can be balanced against the convenience.

The Farmer
Farmers who have hay fields almost always end up with excess hay that they sell off over the course of the year. This method is usually a little cheaper per bale than from the agricultural store. But the more the farmer has to handle the hay, the more expensive it gets per bale.

Off the Field
By far the cheapest way to get hay or haylage is out of the field during the haymaking season. Again, if you have one horse, this can be an easy method – get on the local hay farmer's list, and she or he calls you the morning they are planning to bale. A couple of round trips with a tractor or trailer, and you have your supply.

In order to take full advantage of the off-the-field method, you should have storage space for at least 40–50 bales. If you can get or store only part of what you'll need, at least you will still have paid less for this part than if you got it all from the agricultural store or the farmer's barn in winter.

Delivery
You may also want to consider having your forage delivered during the haymaking season. However, this will cost extra per bale on top of the off-the-field price. If you have more than one or two hay-eating animals and would have to make a million trips back and forth to the field, or you just can't work in the time to pick up your hay, this is a good compromise for getting your year's supply in season.

Farmers advertise hay as 'horse hay', which typically means it is higher quality than what people will buy for other livestock. Some people seem to think it is OK to feed goats mouldy hay, but any hay I buy for any of my animals is high quality, and certainly without mould, dust or mildew.

Some farmers offer to load forage into your barn too, but again it will cost you even more for the workers' time. Some people have hay delivered monthly, which sounds like a nice arrangement; however, you are unlikely to find a supplier who will do this for the amount needed for only one or two horses.

Never lay a plastic tarpaulin over your hay to protect it from rain and roof leaks. While the hay is curing, the plastic will prevent moisture from escaping, and your hay will spoil.

The Haymaking Process in a Nutshell

Hay farmers check their fields regularly for growth. When the growth is sufficient and the weather forecast can confidently predict at least three days of hot, sunny weather, the fields will get cut. The cut hay lays in rows on the ground for two to three days to cure, or dry, during which time it may also be turned once or twice. Then, after a good day of drying in the sun and before the evening dew sets in, the hay is raked, baled and removed from the field, either by customers or the farmer. If the farmer is planning to make haylage, the grass will be baled a day or so earlier and then tightly wrapped in black silage plastic.

Hay Feeding Plan

Any time you can spread your horse's meals into smaller, more frequent ones, it is better for their digestion. However, horse owners usually need to work to support their horse habit, so your horse is probably on the nine-to-five feeding schedule, where he gets fed half his meal in the morning before you go to work, and half in the evening when you get home. While this kind of schedule is not ideal for the digestive function of the horse, thousands of horses survive just fine on it.

Maybe you can find a neighbour to throw your horse a section of hay in the middle of the day, or a responsible child who would love to do that when she gets home from school, in exchange for learning about horses or a small fee. The size of a section of hay can vary almost from bale to bale, but the average-sized horse needs around 2.5 per cent of its body weight in food each day. in winter, at least half of that will be in the form of forage. For a 450kg (1,000lb) horse, that is roughly 5.4–6.75kg (12–15lb) of forage per day.

A horse can deplete a pasture very quickly, eating the grass right down and never giving it enough time to grow again. A rule of thumb for grazing pasture is an acre per horse. Even if you have one horse on one acre, it's best to fence it in half and allow the horse to graze on half for a week or two, then shut that half off and let it grow undisturbed while the horse grazes on the other half.

Hard Feed

In the wild, horses live only on roughage, and they innately know how to get the nutrients they need by seeking out specific herbs and grasses – in other words, horses do not *need* hard feed to thrive. In the domesticated life of the horse, hard feed is more accurately a supplement, making up nutrients that grass or dry forage cannot provide. Hay, haylage or grass should be the main source of nutrition for the horse.

However, horses typically cannot eat enough dry, bulky hay in the course of a day to get the nutrition they need if the hay is of mediocre quality or the horse has a heavy workload. This is where hard feed steps in to fill the nutritional gaps. Most horse owners rely on commercially manufactured horse feeds that have been designed to balance the nutrient intake when fed alongside grass or hay.

Coarse Mix

Coarse mix consists of various grains, and can come with or without molasses. Manufacturers usually have many different combinations in their lines. Often the major difference is in the percentage of protein. Some are actually 'complete' feeds that, if forage is not available, could be fed as the horse's entire ration if given in sufficient quantities.

Organic Coarse Mixes

If you are interested in buying organic coarse mixes, there are a few companies that offer them. As with human food, organic feed is more expensive than non-organic preparations, and if you are interested in feeding wholly organically, you may have difficulty finding organically grown hay. Ask your local agricultural merchant to recommend a brand.

What Kind?

You should pick a brand of coarse mix that is easily available. When you buy your horse, find out what she is eating; if she seems to be doing well with it, you may as well stick to it. If you have other horses or the brand she was eating is not available through your nearby store, you can switch her to a different brand. You will probably find a similar mix in all brands. Always change gradually over the course of a week, mixing the new brand with the old brand, and gradually increasing the amount of the new until you've made a complete switch.

When a Horse Isn't Thriving

If you don't think your horse is thriving on a particular feed, talk with your veterinarian and your feed supplier. They can help you make some decisions about feed choices and help you determine whether a supplement is needed for that individual. In making recommendations, they will consider his breed, size, age, living arrangement and amount of use.

In consultation with your vet, you should rule out certain diseases and illnesses that can contribute to poor digestion. Consider the following:

- Are his teeth in good shape? Get an equine dentist to inspect and file his teeth if necessary. Sharp points develop from uneven wear, making it difficult to chew feed and causing considerable amounts to drop on the ground instead of being ingested by the horse. (See Chapter 3 for a more complete discussion of the horse's teeth.)
- If your horse is eating in a group, is he getting his full ration, or is another horse eating part of his meal?

If your horse gets loose and finds the feed bin, she will happily eat until it is empty. Depending on how much was in the bin, she will almost certainly get colic as a result. A common rule of thumb is to keep feed behind three locks. Lock one might be on the building the feed is kept in, lock two on the feed room door, and lock three on a horseproof feed container (such as a dustbin with a locking lid).

Complete Feeds and Chaffs

Most feed manufacturers offer a feed that contains some roughage and can be fed as a complete feed without hay if fed in sufficient quantities. Alternatively, you can buy chaffs to bulk out your horse's coarse mix ration. These complete feeds are very helpful in maintaining weight and proper nutrition in horses who have health problems such as COPD (a respiratory disease aggravated by the dust in hay – see Chapter 3 for more details), or in older horses whose tooth wear has made chewing hay difficult. Complete feeds often come in pelleted or extruded form (like dog food), but they also can come as loose mixes.

A horse who relies on complete feeds with no hay as her entire ration can be more prone to exhibiting unwanted behaviour, such as chewing wood. This results from the frustration caused by an innate need to eat roughage and simply keep busy.

Weight Control

Both overweight and underweight horses pose health problems. A horse that is slightly underweight is probably better off than an overweight horse. However, it takes very little – illness, overwork – for the slightly underweight individual to become too thin.

Overweight individuals tire easily, and obese brood mares can have breeding difficulties. Some horses, like people, gain weight easily and need to be carefully monitored for food intake. They may need to be taken off pasture and given a more controlled feeding programme. The owner will have to take responsibility for getting the individual the exercise it needs to maintain a good weight. Keep a close eye on your horse's weight, and work with your veterinarian to address any weight issues that arise.

Feeding Differences

The nutritional needs of a growing horse are very different from those of an adult horse who gets light work. Horses need to be fed according to their age and use. All feed manufacturers give recommendations on the bag or in supplemental literature. They also employ nutritionists who will be happy to give you advice over the phone. Following are the typical categories you will find.

Mature, Idle

'Mature' refers to a horse who is beyond growing age. This varies from breed to breed, but is usually around four years old. The idle horse is one who is ridden for only a couple of hours per week and spends the rest of her time hanging around the paddock. This horse does not need to be stuffed full of food, especially in summer. She can often exist on grass alone; however, in winter you might like to give her some coarse mix and possibly some supplements to ensure she is getting enough nutrients in her feed.

Mature, Light Work

An adult horse of five years or older that is ridden for three to five days per week will probably need some hard feed to meet his nutritional needs. Again, in winter you need to be sure of the quality of your hay and consider your horse's individual characteristics to feed him enough but not too much.

Mature, Medium Work

A horse who is ridden for five or six days a week will need to have his hay and/or grass supplemented with a hard feed ration in order to get the proper amount of nutrients.

Mature, Heavy Work

The horse under heavy work, typically a performance horse ridden for a few hours every day and with limited turnout time, will need to be fed hay, coarse mix and probably supplements. Her feeding programme should be carefully constructed and constantly re-evaluated. The type and amount of feed the horse gets will depend on the type of work – jumping, dressage, eventing, hacking – that the horse does.

Brood mares

The brood mare should be fed according to the information just given, except during two critical periods: in the last three months of pregnancy, at which time the foetus is under rapid growth, and while lactating. Otherwise, be sure she is fed with quality hay and coarse mix as needed to supplement the quality of the hay. During the last three months of pregnancy, her need for protein, calcium and phosphorus increases dramatically, and these will probably need to be given to her as a supplement, rather than simply by increasing her overall hard feed ration. Continue the same sort of regimen while the mare is lactating, but pay particular attention to the mare's decrease in lactation. As the foal heads towards weaning (in two to three months), begin to decrease the mare's feed accordingly.

The Growing Horse

Nursing foals, weanlings, and yearlings all need access to high-quality hay; often need to be fed hard feed to supplement hay or grass; and may need supplements beyond that. Like all horses, these youngsters will need 24-hour access to fresh water and mineralized salt.

Many plants and flowers are poisonous to horses, including rhododendron, foxglove, laurel, yew, deadly nightshade, bracken, ragwort, buttercup, lily of the valley, narcissus and larkspur. If you see a sudden onset of diarrhoea, colic, extensive salivation, staggering or muscle weakness, or if the horse collapses, call your vet immediately.

Supplements

Look in any equine supply catalogue or tack shop, and the array of supplements you will find can be mind-boggling. The catalogue copy sounds appealing, and you can easily go a little overboard. You can also drain your bank account paying for these supplements and add a lot of complications to feeding time by having to pull one from a multitude of supplement buckets.

Consult Your Team

As with all other health and nutrition concerns with your horse, turn to your horse's health care team – the veterinarian, holistic practitioner, farrier, feed suppliers and you – to determine what, if anything, your horse might need for supplements.

Salt Blocks

Salt and mineral blocks come in small brick-like sizes or large blocks. If you feed commercial coarse mix, your horse will probably get all the appropriate trace minerals she needs, so you could choose to use plain white salt blocks. Hang one in every horse's stable and keep one in the paddock so that horses can always have free access to salt, which is a key mineral in their diet. If at all possible, keep larger blocks under some sort of cover, since they will deteriorate fast when rained on.

How to Feed Supplements

Most supplements come in pelleted form and are added to the horse's daily feed ration. (For 'natural' nutritional supplements, see Chapter 10.)

What does choke mean?
This is a condition that is often caused when a horse gulps down its hard feed too rapidly and the food gets stuck in its oesophagus. To deter this, place a couple of stones in the feed bucket – having to eat around them makes the horse slow down.

Multivitamins

All vitamins except A and E are made by bacteria in the horse's intestines. Only A and E need to be supplied through the diet, so giving multivitamins to a healthy, properly fed animal is probably overkill.

B Vitamins

B vitamins are often given to animals who are stressed and who are showing weight loss and lack of vigour. B vitamins are available in quick-dissolving gel-and-paste form in an oral syringe.

Vitamin C

As with vitamin B, horses make their own vitamin C and do not need to supplement this antioxidant unless they have a chronic illness.

Supplements for Older Horses

Most supplements directed at older horses are to relieve arthritis and joint pain, and include a glucosamine/chondroitin mix for joint flexibility (a typical brand name is Cortaflex). Some are digestive aids and include bacterial cultures, such as acidophilus, that are critical to digestion, since older horses often don't process their food as efficiently as they did when they were younger.

Mare and Foal Supplements

Most of these are basically multivitamins with electrolytes and trace minerals to boost levels in growing horses and lactating mares.

Hoof Growth Supplements

The horse's hoof is important. If the hoof is not growing properly, it probably wouldn't hurt to add a supplement to the horse's diet. However, as always, consult your equine health care team, especially your veterinarian and farrier, to determine the need of supplementation of this kind. Hoof problems may also be caused by environmental factors, and it may be the daily care that needs to be altered, not the horse's nutrition.

Calcium and Phosphorus

Calcium and phosphorus are extremely important to the health of a horse. However, they are also dependent on each other, and their ratio is as important as their quantity. The perfect ratio is between 1:1 and 3:1, calcium to phosphorus, but should always consist of at least as much calcium as phosphorus.

Coat Supplements

These are supplements intended to enhance coat shine and maintenance, and are usually fortified with fatty acids as well as the usual vitamins and minerals.

Respiratory Supplements

These are supplements intended to help with respiratory problems. They range from cough syrup-like formulas to mixes of herbs and herbal extracts for nutritional support for horses with conditions that cause coughing and breathing problems.

Vitamin E and Selenium

These two nutrients are best given in combination. Too much selenium is toxic, but not enough can cause muscle deficiencies and a weakened immune system.

Keep it Simple

There are many more supplements and types of feeding and feeding programmes that you will run across as you get more experience with horses. Always keep in mind that the horse's natural diet is quite simple. If you can keep your feed programme simple while getting the horse the nutrition she needs, you will both be much happier.

CHAPTER 8

Grooming

Grooming your horse is good for both her physical and mental health. It is a great way to interact with your horse in an enjoyable activity, as well as giving you the opportunity to check her over for nicks and cuts, skin problems and other things you might not see unless you get your hands on her. You don't need to groom your horse every day – although simple grooming is one thing you can't really overdo!

Your horse will really appreciate it if you retrieve her from her paddock and just groom her instead of always retrieving her only to make her go to work. Grooming a horse is also great exercise for you.

Grooming and Riding

It is necessary to brush the dirt out of your horse's coat and to pick her feet both before and after you ride – regardless of whether your ride consists of schooling in the arena or a hack out on the bridle paths. Brushing the coat where the saddle will come in contact with it is critical, but it is also important to clean the dirt out of the rest of the horse's coat as well, since the dirt will irritate her skin when she gets sweaty from exercise.

On your return from a ride, you may want to hose your horse down in the summer season. However, just use water; bathing her with shampoos after every ride can be detrimental to her coat. If it's not the right season for hosing off sweat, at least wipe your horse down with a towel in the sweaty areas and wipe off any mud or wetness from snow, puddles or wet roads. Wipe her face and ears down with a damp towel too, since she will be itchy in those places. Take a few extra minutes to give her back a bit of a rubdown – your horse will definitely appreciate it. Once the sweaty areas are dry, brush her coat out thoroughly.

If you show your horse, expect to become an expert at grooming. Competition in the horse-show world is stiff, and you will want to give your horse every little edge to stand out from the crowd. Perfect grooming with every detail attended to is just one more point in your favour on the judge's card. Even if grooming isn't an official aspect of a particular class, it never hurts to have the judge look favourably upon your team.

Grooming Tools

First, you should set up some sort of box with the basic grooming tools you need to give your horse an average grooming. Inexpensive boxes come in heavy-duty plastic of all colours. (If you have more than one horse and want to keep their grooming tools separate, you can colour-coordinate each individual box and brushes.)

Cotton socks with worn heels and deteriorated elastic, or whose partner has been mysteriously eaten by the tumble-drier, make handy items to have in the yard – I keep a plastic grocery bag full of socks hanging in my tack room. You can dampen them and use them to wipe your horse's face and ears; clean boots with them; use them to wipe down the bit after a ride – the list is endless. Keep a second bag, bucket or basket to throw the dirty ones into. When your supply of clean worn socks starts to get low, throw the dirty load in the laundry. If a sock is exceptionally soiled, just throw it away.

Another handy thing to have is a grooming apron or overalls, which will protect your clothing from getting covered in horsehair, dust and mud. If you get an apron with pockets in the front, it will be handy for holding brushes, a hoof pick or plaiting equipment.

Brushes

Curry Comb

Curry combs are typically made of stiff rubber, with a ring of pointed edges around the outside. They are used to brush the surface mud off your horse's coat. These brushes come in round or oval shapes and are designed to be used in a gentle circular motion. Metal or plastic curry combs should be used to clean dandy brushes (see below) – never use a metal curry comb on your horse.

You can pick up very inexpensive horse brushes. But if you can, or maybe once you get beyond your starting purchases, buy good-quality natural-hair brushes. Nice brushes make the task of grooming that much more pleasant for both you and the horse.

Dandy Brush

A dandy brush is made of quite stiff fibres designed to really get down to the skin and brush dirt to the surface. Be careful not to get a brush with bristles that are too stiff, however; you're dealing with an animal that can feel a fly land on its rear, so imagine how a really stiff brush feels! Instead, get a brush that's stiff but flexible, and learn to use the flick of a wrist to get loose dirt to the surface.

Body Brush

This brush is the last you'll use in your grooming routine. It is very soft and used to brush away the loose dirt while leaving a polished shine to your horse's coat.

Face Brush

Brushes for the face are very soft and come in different sizes. You will want a fairly small one to do the delicate areas around your horse's nose, eyes and ears.

Mane/Tail Brushes

Mane and tail hair grows very slowly, so you should be careful to pull out as little as possible. If the mane or tail becomes knotted, use one of the products described in the next section to loosen the knots before you run a brush through the hair.

Keep all your basic tools handy for grooming before riding. Fill a box or bucket, or hang a wire basket near the place you tack up with basics, such as a curry comb, hoof pick, brushes, mane/tail brush and towel.

Hoof Picks

There are a few different kinds of hoof picks. They are relatively inexpensive, so you can try out different kinds and see which suits you best. My personal favourite is the kind with a thick plastic handle and a stiff brush on the other side of the hoof pick. The brush allows you to brush mud and dirt off the horse's hoof before picking it up, and to brush off the remnants of what you pick out of the hoof.

Simple hoof picks come as steel picks with vinyl-coated handles of different colours. Also common are hoof picks in a pocket-knife style; these fold in half and are handy to carry in your pocket.

Clippers

If your horse gets a thick winter coat, or you want to work her hard through the winter, you may want to clip off some of her winter coat. Make sure you buy clippers that are intended for horses. They need to be sturdy and suitable for a horse's coat and mane hair. Have extra blades handy, since clipping coarse hair dulls the blades quickly.

To get your horse used to clippers, first let her see them, check them out, smell them and feel them. Turn them on and let her hear them from a distance. If she is handling all this well, she may be ready to feel them against her skin while they are on.

Normally, it would be best to have your horse on a lead rope for this kind of thing, and to let her move as much as she needs to. It also helps to use cordless clippers initially, so that you can easily move with the horse when she moves. When she stops moving, take the clippers away to let her know that standing still was what you were looking for. Then slowly start again, working with the places on her body where she is OK with the clippers and moving to less comfortable areas gradually. It's worth taking your time over this; once your horse is comfortable with clippers, she should remain so.

If you plan to clip your horse's ears, make sure you use clippers of an appropriate small size and get your horse totally comfortable with having her ears handled before you start trying to clip them.

There are different levels of clipping, and the level you choose depends on how hard your horse will work in the winter, how cold the winters are in your area, how much rugging up you want to do, and how much you want your horse to go outside in the winter. Types of clipping include:

- **Trace clip:** Just the areas on the lower part of the body from the middle of the side to the top of the legs are clipped.
- **Blanket clip:** A rug-like area of unclipped hair is left on the horse's back from the withers to the croup.

- **Hunter clip:** The entire body is clipped except an outline of the saddle. (Position the saddle or saddle pad on the horse's back to act as a template while clipping.)

If you bathe and groom your horse to prepare him for a show the following day, bed the stable with fresh shavings and rug him with a light stable rug. If you clip your horse, you will need to rug him accordingly – for example, a full body clip in winter means heavier rugging, both indoors and out. Rugging also gives you a few other things to consider while grooming – for example, you need to watch for sore and chafed areas where the rug may have rubbed the horse.

Other Tools

Shedding Blades

If your horse is allowed to grow a nice winter coat, you should have a shedding blade around to help you in the spring when that coat really starts to shed. The traditional shedding blade comes as a long, thin metal blade with a leather handle on either end that can be folded and hooked to make a loop. The blade is smooth on one edge, and has small teeth on the other to get loose hair out.

A shedding and mud tool that is also useful is a flat rubber mitten with little bumps on both sides. This gentle tool lifts mud and loose hair, and you can really scrub at the mud without hurting your horse.

Towels and Wipes

Always have some clean towels around the yard. They are useful for any number of things, from grooming to first aid. White towels are good to have around for first aid use, since the dye in coloured towels is probably not good for open cuts. A roll of paper towels and moisturized hand wipes also come in handy.

What does hogging mean?
Hogging refers to a mane that has been completely shaved.

Bathing Items

Horses shouldn't be shampooed too often (although for the show ring, it's almost inevitable that they will be bathed regularly), but when you do choose to bathe your horse, there is a wealth of products to choose from. Shampoos can be moisturizing, can include a bracer that feels good after a hard workout, or can be conditioning and intended to make your horse's coat shine like never before. Some shampoos are specifically antifungal; others include fly-repellant products such as citronella. Shampoos also exist especially for grey and white horse coats.

Rubber mitt-style brushes are great for shampooing. They have short bristles on one side, hard rubber bumps on the other, and a hole on either side at the opening of the mitt that allows you to stick your thumb through to better hold the mitt.

Plaiting

Plaiting styles depend on the discipline – and, in fact, the need to plait at all depends on the discipline – but it can be a fun thing to do, whether or not you compete. In general, the more plaits you put in a mane, the longer the neck appears to be. Just a few thick plaits make the neck appear shorter and thicker. Mane plaits can be left hanging, tucked up into themselves in neat little bobs, or looped into the next plait in chain-like links. Plaited manes are traditionally accompanied by plaited tails, which can be left in one thick, long plait or woven into tight, smaller plaits.

Sweat Scrapers

Something as simple as a sweat scraper comes in various styles. First, you can choose between plastic or aluminium. There's also a squeegee-style sweat scraper similar to the type you use on your windscreen, only curved. As with many things with horses, you will need to use a few different kinds to discover what suits you best.

Grooming Products

Many products exist to make grooming a little easier. Some just smell nice and make the horse look more polished; others have very practical purposes, such as detangling manes or making plaiting easier. Most of these products are available in a few different brands, the main difference often being smell. They can be expensive, so you may want to ask friends what they are using, then make some choices of what to try and what you definitely aren't interested in before you make any purchases.

Mane/Tail Detanglers

These detanglers do their job well, and they usually smell great. They generally come in spray form. Be aware that the spray is so slippery that you need to be careful not to get any on the saddle area. If you get it on your hands, you will find it difficult to keep reins from slipping through your fingers.

Coat Gloss

Coat gloss is used to make your horse's coat shine. Glosses are topical enhancements only and don't have any deep-seated effects on coat health. For more lasting effects, you need to find supplements designed specifically for that purpose.

Hoof Dressings

Horses in the show ring have their toenails polished. Black has always been available, but now you can choose copper, silver, sparkling and many other colours of hoof! Be careful that the product you choose doesn't have a drying effect, especially if you choose to remove it with hoof polish remover. Ask your farrier her or his opinion, especially if your horse has less than perfect hoofs to begin with. As with any product, if used excessively, hoof dressing may cause problems.

Grooming How-To's

Body

To give your horse's coat a thorough grooming, follow these steps:

1. Begin with a curry comb of your choosing and brush up loose hair and underlying dirt. If the horse is moulting, use a shedding blade first and get as much loose hair as possible out before you begin brushing. Use these tools only on the horse's main body, not in areas where bones stick out, such as in the flank or shoulder area, and not on the legs and face.
2. Use your stiffest dandy brush to brush out all the loose dirt and hair that the curry comb brought to the surface. Use this brush to get the mud off the horse's legs. Don't forget under the mane. Brush gently but firmly, using a flicking motion as the brush leaves the horse's body to help lift up deeply embedded dirt.
3. Use the soft body brush to brush out any remaining hair and dirt and to give your horse's coat a nice shine.
4. Finish by rubbing down your horse's coat with a clean, soft towel.

As you groom your horse, look for cuts, parasites or other skin problems. Be aware of any tenderness he may exhibit as you brush him. While picking out his hooves, look for any bruises or sensitivity in that area, especially if you picked out a stone or stick that was caught in his foot.

Hooves

Pick out your horse's hooves both before and after riding. Doing so before you ride allows you to pick out anything that might bother the horse's feet on the ride. Doing so after riding allows you to examine the hoof and remove any stones or pieces of sticks, or anything else that the horse may have picked up and got stuck in its hoof while out on the ride.

Reserve a small, fairly stiff brush (maybe one of those cheap ones that you bought with your starter set of grooming supplies that has since been replaced with a high-quality natural bristle brush) to remove the dirt and mud from the outside of the hoof.

Pick up a foot and use your hoof pick to gently dig the packed dirt, manure and bedding out of the grooves (bars) around the triangular-shaped protrusion known as the frog. If your horse is shoeless, the rest of the dirt will pop out. If your horse has shoes on, which he probably does, then you will also need to remove other packed dirt that has stuck to the inside of the shoe.

Plaiting

If you are as inept with hair styling as I am, buy yourself a little plaiting kit that comes with rubber bands and a three-pronged fork that splits the hair into three even sections for easier plaiting. The kits are available at most tack shops, are inexpensive, and come with instructions.

Bathing

First, if your horse isn't properly halter-broken (see Chapter 11), you might as well forget about a bath and spend your time doing some groundwork. Good halter-breaking is critical for introducing things such as hoses to horses. You should understand how to let your horse move and at the same time be able to direct that movement to support her and help her understand that the hose is harmless. If you can't do this, you are wasting your time and making things more stressful than they need to be.

I don't condone shaving your horse's whiskers, but if you're going to show your horse, especially in-hand, you will need to succumb to this practice. You can use small electric clippers designed for delicate areas; some people use disposable human razors, especially for touch-ups. Don't shave the inside of his ears; this hair keeps out dirt, water and insects. If his ear hair is long and unruly, you can tidy it up with a small pair of scissors.

If you plan to bathe your horse for the first time, don't just turn the hose on her. As with anything new to a horse, take the time to introduce it to her slowly. In so doing, you will save her some stress and save time in the long run. Get a long amount of hose out. If you have a hose attachment that offers different spray types, choose one that is shower-like – you don't want to drill holes through the horse, though you do want her to feel the water.

Turn the water on just a bit and begin by spraying the ground near her. Don't do this long enough to frighten her, just to let her know that this 'thing' exists; spray the water on her feet and lower legs and let her know that this noisy thing isn't going to hurt her. Keep working up the body, staying at each level until she accepts it. It may take a few sessions, but if you introduce the hose gradually and in a manner fitting to her, she will come to enjoy bath time.

If you aren't using a hose to bathe your horse, assemble the things you will need to bathe her – buckets of warm water, brushes, a sweat scraper, and, depending on the temperature, a light rug – before you get your horse on the scene. Where you bathe your horse depends on your set-up. Most large livery yards will have a specific area. If you are lucky, there may even be heated water available.

You will find it a bit difficult to get a dry horse's coat wet – the way water runs off is proof in action of how well-designed horses are to withstand the elements! Once you get her wet, squeeze a thin line of shampoo along her body and give her a little shampoo massage. Do one side at a time and rinse it thoroughly before moving on to the other side – leaving shampoo behind to dry into your horse's coat is worse than never having bathed her at all.

The best way to get soap out is to use a hose directly on your horse. Once the horse is thoroughly rinsed, start on her upper body and use the sweat scraper to scrape the excess water off. When you wash the horse's face, use warm water (no soap), a flannel and a little elbow grease. Never get water down a horse's ears.

CHAPTER 9

General Health

Horses seem to be at once very healthy and very delicate. A constant supply of water, quality hay and hard feed when appropriate, combined with lots of turnout time, preferably on grass, does more to keep a horse in good health than almost anything else you can do. The well-maintained horse can withstand hot summer or cold winter temperatures, and the physical conditions under which they can thrive range from cushy double-glazed stables to a three-sided shed right in the middle of a rocky pasture.

But when things go wrong, they can go wrong in a big way. The more you do to prevent horse health problems, the less it will cost the horse in stress and potential lifelong health issues, and the less it will cost you in both time and money.

The Horse's Environment

Chapters 6 and 7 offer a lot of information about keeping your horse healthy. Here are some key environmental factors that also contribute to the general good health of your horse:

· Pick manure from stables and turnout areas at least once per day – more often if there are more than two horses out together. Horses who stand in accumulated manure and breathe in urine odours are susceptible to hoof diseases, chronic respiratory problems, parasite infestations and a host of other secondary problems.

· Keep areas clear of debris and fences in good repair to avoid physical injury to your horse. Horses can get into enough trouble on their own without your contribution. Fix damaged items – loose fence boards, damaged or broken electric fence wire, protruding nails – as soon as you see them. If you don't, your horse will surely find them, and that will lead to the most devastating consequences.

· Lock up feed and keep stored hay out of your horse's reach if possible. Close off any areas that aren't safe for a horse to walk in, and keep such areas free of tempting things, such as hay bales, which will lure them into that area.

· Use fencing and equipment designed for horses. Never underestimate the strength of a horse, especially one who leans all his weight on a fence to scratch his itchy behind.

· If something seems a little dangerous, it is – and it is ten times more dangerous when you add a horse to the picture!

Learn About Good Health for Horses

Start by reading this book, of course. But you will also want a few references on hand in the event that your horse seems ill. (See Appendix A for a list of horse health manuals.) Although you should always call a vet when your horse is not well, you should also have something to refer to before the vet arrives.

Your Horse Care Team

I believe in assembling a diverse team of equine-knowledgeable people to help you with your horse's care. This team has many members, including you, at least one equine veterinarian, a farrier, an equine dentist, a holistic practitioner, the stable manager if you keep your horse at livery, and your group of horse-owning friends.

You

You are the most important person on your horse's team. You not only administer the most care to your horse – preventive and recuperative – but also pick the other team members, so the success of your team is largely on your shoulders. You know your horse the best, especially if you keep him at home, and you choose when and if to call in those other team members.

It is rare for money not to be a factor in making decisions about horse care. It is up to you to decide the level of expense you can handle for your horse and the different horse-related things that may come up. It can be a good use of funds to spend some money up front to educate yourself in equine health, nutrition and first aid; this is a good way to save yourself from having to call the vet for every little malady but still be able to do the right thing by your horse.

www.horseit.com is a nicely designed website with lots of good basic horsey information and a number of useful links.

Veterinarian

Your choice of veterinarian may be limited to who is local to you. If you have a few options, you are fortunate; you may find that each practitioner has an area – for example, reproduction or surgery – that he or she tends to be more specialized in. You should have one veterinarian who will come to know your horses.

Farrier

Perhaps your farrier will spend most of his or her time simply putting shoes on your horse. However, health problems with the foot can be common, and you should have a farrier who is willing to respond to an emergency and who is knowledgeable in foot health as well as in nailing on a shoe. Most people doing farrier work for a profession have educated themselves in foot health as well as shoeing – in fact, the equine veterinarian's education consists of very few hours on the foot, unless it is the student's speciality area.

Your farrier will be a critical member of your horse's health team. You will see the farrier for general maintenance more regularly than any other member of the team – on an average of once every six to eight weeks. It's important to find someone who you can work well with and whose approach to your horse matches your own.

Equine Dentist

All equine veterinarians are knowledgeable about the horse's teeth in terms of general maintenance and wear and tear. But the teeth are second in importance only to the foot. And just as you wouldn't expect, ask or even want your veterinarian to trim and shoe your horse, it makes sense that neither would you ask him or her to examine and work on her teeth. A sound practice might be to have your veterinarian check and 'float' your horse's teeth (that is, rasp away sharp points) in the spring when he or she administers spring vaccinations. Then in autumn you can make an appointment with an equine dentist who can also be used for any special problems throughout the rest of the year.

Although the practice of equine dentistry is becoming more common, equine dentists are not widespread; the ones that are out there are usually extremely busy. Start your search before the need for one arises. Let the dentist get accustomed to your horse with a maintenance check; don't wait for a dental emergency to find a dentist and introduce your horse to dentistry for the first time.

Holistic Practitioner

If you are interested in using homeopathy, herbs, energy therapies such as Reiki, massage, acupressure and acupuncture in your horse care programme, you should find a knowledgeable practitioner (and probably more than one) to join your health care team. Read more about this in Chapter 10.

Stable Manager

If you keep your horse at livery, the person who feeds or leads your horse out to the paddock and back to her stable every day will know a lot about your horse's normal behaviour and when she is acting abnormally. He or she may be your first line of defence when it comes to realizing that your horse needs health care.

Horse Friends

The group of friends with whom you ride will also be an important part of your team. They are the ones to speak to, to exchange information about a new feed or a place to buy bedding, or any of the other ins and outs of owning a horse. They will be your moral support when your horse is ill or lame, and while you are working through the sometimes complex process of figuring out just what is wrong. In return, you will be an important part of their horse care team as well.

Finding a Veterinarian

Find a local large-animal veterinarian before you even bring your first horse home. It's nice to have an established relationship with the vet who has been to your place for routine vaccinations and so on, before you need him or her to come in an emergency situation. If you don't have a horse trailer or the horse can't be transported, it will be comforting to know that the vet already has some idea of how to get to your place.

Finding an equine veterinarian shouldn't be too difficult in most parts of the country. You can simply look in the Yellow Pages.

If you don't find a large animal veterinary practice listed, call a small-animal practice and ask for a referral, or ask friends to recommend one.

Once you locate a vet or two, you should get some feedback from horse owners who have used that practice. Go to a place with horses and ask who they use, or whether they know about a particular vet. Alternatively, go to a large livery yard and ask there. Don't ask just one person, however; ask at least three so that you can compare experiences and come to your own conclusion.

After you make a choice, phone his or her office and ask if you can come to see the surgery (there will probably be a yard set up for surgery and follow-up care). How these enquiries are handled can tell you a lot about the practice.

> Here are the four important vital statistics to know about the horse:
>
> 1. Temperature: about 38.5° C (100–101° F)
> 2. Pulse: 30–40 beats per minute
> 3. Respiration: 8–20 breaths per minute
> 4. Capillary refill time (CRT): 1–2 seconds for blood to return to blanched tissue
>
> While these statistics are average for the mature horse, you should establish a set of figures that is normal for your horse.

If everything sounds good on the phone, pay a visit to the surgery. You should find a neat, clean facility with professional staff who know how to answer your questions. If the first visit by the vet to your yard goes well and all other things work out, you've got yourself the beginning of a long-term relationship.

Establish a Baseline

If you have just bought your horse, you may have had a vet check performed (see Chapter 5). The results of this exam can give you a baseline with which you can begin to know your horse's health – it's a standard from which she may veer off. The results of the check should give you a temperature, respiration and pulse report.

Don't attack your horse with a rectal thermometer the minute you get her home, but do learn how to perform such procedures so that you know how to do them and your horse will be accustomed to them before she is actually ill. The best way to keep your horse healthy is to get to know her inside and out.

Vaccinations

Annual vaccinations are the most basic part of health maintenance. These include tetanus and influenza. Herpes viruses can also be vaccinated against at the same time.

Tetanus

Horses are very susceptible to tetanus, and their environment – old stables, rusty nails, manure – readily supports this bacteria, which affects the nervous system and for which successful treatment is difficult at best. There is an effective annual vaccination for tetanus. If your horse suffers a deep puncture wound, your vet may administer a booster tetanus vaccine at the time of the trauma.

Equine Herpes Virus

Herpes virus is spread by carrier horses who may be symptomless. There are four main herpes viruses in horses, and they are widespread. The most noticeable symptoms of EHV-1, EHV-2 and EHV-3 are respiratory problems, such as discharge from the nostrils and coughing. EHV-1 can induce abortions in severe cases. Mating is a common cause of the spread of EHV-3 and often produces fever when spread this way. In rare cases, EHV-4 can cause loss of coordination and paralysis. EHV-1 can be vaccinated against, but there is no fully effective treatment for the other types, although antibiotics help with secondary infections. The majority of horses recover from EHV, although it takes time and careful nursing.

It is up to you to halter-break your horse thoroughly enough for him to be gentle to handle. A vet should be able to give your horse a simple physical check, administer annual vaccinations and draw blood without difficulty. However, don't let any practitioner handle your horse in a way you don't approve of.

Strangles

This inflammation of the upper respiratory tract causes swollen lymph nodes that often abscess and break, contaminating the area and making other horses susceptible. Strangles is highly contagious and hearty, making a horse infectious for as long as a month. Vaccinations may soon become available against strangles.

What is azoturia?
Also known as 'tying up' or 'Monday morning disease', **azoturia** refers to the cramping of a horse's large muscles.

Healthy Teeth

The condition of a horse's teeth is critical to his overall well-being. The domesticated horse is fed in such a way that he does not wear his teeth evenly, as he would in the wild while grazing on pasture all the time – and add to that having to hold a bit in his mouth. By domesticating such an animal, we have made ourselves responsible for some things that nature would normally take care of. (See Chapter 3 for a section on the anatomy of the horse's mouth and tooth structure.)

It is important to have an equine dentist look at your horse, but dentists are very busy and expensive. I take a two-step approach:

1. When I have my horse vaccinated, I ask my regular equine veterinarian to check my horses' teeth for sharp edges and loose caps. Tooth maintenance is always important for good digestion.

2. In the autumn, before we go into the winter, I have my horses' teeth checked again by an equine dentist; that way I can be sure that the extra feed I am starting to give them to keep warm in winter is going to be used efficiently.

In order to effectively examine the horse's teeth, your practitioner will use a speculum. Speculums come in many designs, and all serve to keep the horse's mouth wide open so that a thorough visual and manual examination can take place and teeth can be easily reached.

The dental speculum is used to prop open the horse's mouth for inspection of the teeth and mouth, and to perform work on the teeth. Speculums are usually made of metal and are held open in a variety of ways. Expect your equine dentist to use one to do a proper examination.

You should be prepared with a couple of buckets of warm water for rinsing tools and rinsing the horse's mouth during dental work. The most common thing the dentist may find in the examination are sharp edges that have been created by uneven wear of the teeth. These can make it difficult to chew and cause inefficient digestion of feed; they can also cause ulcerations of the mouth lining that cause the horse to lose interest in eating.

Lameness

The causes of lameness can be external or internal. The centre of the problem is usually in either the leg or the foot. You may or may not know what caused the lameness. Common lameness problems are typically seen in horses who are subject to a lot of foot stresses, such as abrupt changes in direction, landing from jumps and so on, as well as in overweight horses. Navicular disease is something horse owners dread. It causes changes in the tissues and supporting structure of the small navicular bone in the foot. A farrier can help make the horse more comfortable.

Although horses can be used once they have developed navicular disease, such use is often limited.

Obvious Causes

If a horse suddenly becomes lame, the first place to look at is the foot. Check the foot on the lame leg for a nail, stick or stone. If nothing is there, begin to check the rest of the leg for tender spots, swelling or warmth, which is a sign of inflammation. At the tender site, look for an abrasion or puncture wound. An abrasion would probably have to be significant and, therefore, very visible to cause lameness, but puncture wounds can be extremely deep and hard to detect. A puncture wound as high as the shoulder could cause lameness as well.

You may have seen your horse fall, get a leg caught under or in a fence, go through an unsafe wooden structure or fall getting out of the horse trailer. Although these accidents can cause serious and even permanent lameness, sometimes it is a comfort to at least know what the cause was.

Minor lameness from obvious causes is fairly manageable. If you saw the incident happen, administering arnica (see Chapter 10) immediately can be very effective. However, its effectiveness is thought to be lessened as time passes. So if you didn't see a crash, misstep or fall, it may be too late for arnica to help significantly (although it won't hurt, either). You might want to administer phenylbutazone – also known as bute – an anti-inflammatory pain reliever, for a day or two to help relieve the horse's pain. However, bute is a drug and needs to be prescribed by your veterinarian, who will want to see the horse first. The thing to be careful of with bute and other pain-masking drugs is that they can make the horse feel well enough to move around too much. If the horse can remain calm in his stable for a day or two, bute combined with limited mobility may be all that is needed.

Mystery Lamenesses

If a mystery lameness doesn't respond to bute and stable rest within a day or two, call the vet again. Make sure the bute has passed through the system

– it normally takes 24 hours – and that the lameness is evident again by the time the vet comes, so that he can see the lameness in action.

Lameness is a serious issue under the best of circumstances, but when you have no idea what has caused it, getting your veterinarian on the scene as soon as possible can make the difference between a short-term lay-up and chronic lameness. Your vet may want to take X-rays or perform a nerve block test to zoom in on the real issue.

To pinpoint lameness problems, your vet may want to administer a nerve block test. This diagnostic tool numbs an area of the leg to see if the lameness disappears when the horse cannot feel pain from the affected area.

Laminitis

Like colic, laminitis is one of the things horse owners hear about a lot. Laminitis is an inflammation of the laminae – the interlocking sensitive tissues surrounded by the horn – in the foot. It is typically used interchangeably with the term 'founder', but founder is actually a result of laminitis that has progressed enough for the coffin bone to rotate, resulting in a chronic condition caused by permanent structural damage. Horses who have foundered can be kept fairly comfortable through drugs and corrective shoeing, but they will only be able to withstand extremely light riding, if any at all.

Common causes of laminitis are overeating on lush pasture and postpartum infection of the mare, both of which cause enterotoxemia. Below are the signs of laminitis:

· Hot feet caused by increased circulation.
· Rapid pulse in foot area.
· Preference for lying down to take weight off feet, when all four feet are involved.
· Leaning back on the hind end to relieve the front feet, or holding the front legs out in an odd stretched position, if just the two front feet are involved.

Laminitis and founder are conditions that will require your farrier and veterinarian to work together to treat the horse.

Colic – the Equine 'C Word'

While horses do get cancer, the frightening 'C word' in the horse world is colic. Almost everything you do for your horse has some effect on the horse's potential for colic. Feeding schedule, food storage, the feed itself, access to fresh water, stress, hard riding, no exercise, transporting, administering medications, feeding on the ground, escaping and overeating – you name it, and colic can be the result!

What is Colic?

Colic is simply a stomach ache. It can be many different kinds of stomach ache – windy, not windy, causing diarrhoea or causing constipation. But what may simply be a stomach ache in many other animals is a life-threatening condition for the horse.

Colic is not a disease in and of itself, but a symptom of some other problem. It may be an external factor, such as overeating or bad feed, or it may be caused by something internally such as a strong heat cycle in a mare, a parasite infestation or even a tumour. The cause may be obvious – you found your horse in the feed room halfway through what was a full bag of grain. But if it is something less obvious, it can be difficult to find the cause. If the cause is chronic, either colic will occur again or some other symptom will arise.

What are the Signs of Colic?

The signs of colic can be many; this is where it is important to come to know your horse's usual behaviour. Being a picky eater can be a normal thing for one horse but a colic warning sign in another horse who normally eats with relish. Other things to watch for include the horse not passing manure, grabbing at her sides with her mouth or kicking at her stomach with her back legs, exhibiting restlessness in her stable, sweating excessively for no apparent reason (such as hard work or extremely hot temperatures), lying down for a long period of time and not getting up when you encourage her, or rolling.

What do you do for a Colicky Horse?

The first thing to do is alert your veterinarian. If you have just started to see signs of colic, you may not think a visit is necessary yet. However, your vet will want to be on the scene as soon as possible – addressing colic immediately can mean the difference between a simple stomach ache and a life-threatening situation.

If the horse is not passing manure, first try getting the horse out and walking around. This will serve to keep the horse from lying down or rolling. If the horse's stomach is impacted with feed that won't pass through, rolling can cause the intestine to twist, which is absolutely to be avoided. In a mild colic episode, getting the horse moving can stimulate her system to cause her to pass manure.

Another strategy is to load the horse into a horse trailer. This can be just the stimulation he needs. Even though my mare walks calmly into a trailer, she is still on edge and almost immediately passes manure when she gets in. If your horse does not load well, even simply asking him to load can be enough. However, if your horse is really afraid of getting into a trailer, do not add this stress to the already existing stress of colic.

Pain-relieving medications and antispasmodics can be administered to relieve the pain of wind colic, and can help relax the muscles enough to help the horse release wind and/or manure and relieve the colic episode.

Here are some questions your vet is likely to ask during an exam for colic:
- When was the last time the horse ate?
- Has the horse been loose? If so, what might she have eaten?
- Is the horse passing manure?
- What is the horse's temperature?
- Is she nervous and pacing, or standing in a corner hanging her head?
- Is she lying down a lot? Has she rolled?
- Is she grabbing or kicking at her sides?

Chapter 10 covers other treatments you can administer while waiting for the vet to arrive. Reiki, massage and other energy therapies can help relieve the colic and relax the horse, and make him more comfortable while waiting for an assessment of the situation.

Worming

Because they eat from the ground and often on less than lush pasture, horses are subject to being robbed of nutrition and having their digestive tract damaged by many different kinds of parasitic worms. Your veterinarian can suggest a worming programme. Alternatively, ask for advice at your local agricultural store.

The best defence against worms is prevention. Clean manure out of the horse's area as often as possible. Of course, it isn't feasible to stand behind the horse with a manure fork, but picking out stables daily and paddocks once or twice a day is ideal. Fresh manure is the perfect environment for flies to lay their eggs, which, if left in the paddock, can be ingested by the horse.

Below are the most problematic worms that affect horses:

- **Roundworms:** these can cause intestinal blockage if the build-up is large, but regular worming typically keeps the population within tolerable levels.
- **Small and large strongyles:** these are bloodsucking worms of the roundworm group that attach themselves to the intestine and can cause anaemia, ulcers and colic.
- **Tapeworms:** these are common in horses. They steal nutrients and, like any worm infestation, large numbers can cause anaemia, wasting and colic.
- **Bots:** Bot flies lay little yellow eggs on the horse's body; the eggs are ingested and cycle through the body, passing out through the manure, where the fly emerges and the cycle repeats itself. Like all worms, they are nutrient robbers in high quantities. The adult flies are a nuisance around horses, who don't tend to like them.

· **Lungworms:** Rare in horses but usually associated with donkeys, lungworms live in the lungs.

The best thing to do is have a sample of your horse's manure tested, and then worm accordingly. A simple, inexpensive test will detect most worms, but tapeworms and a few others can be detected only by a more expensive test, whose results take longer to return. Most horse owners find this cumbersome and simply administer a scheduled worming programme, usually every other month. Don't neglect this important aspect of your horse's health, or instead of feeding your horse, you'll be feeding a parasite population.

To treat worms, most people use paste wormers that come in syringe-like tubes. All you have to do is spin the little dial up to the proper weight for your horse and administer the appropriate amount of paste onto the back of the horse's tongue.

Avoid administering paste wormers around mealtimes. The thick paste stays in the horse's mouth for a while before it all dissolves and is swallowed. If the horse has access to hay after getting a mouthful of paste, he can use the hay to cleanse his palette by spitting out the worm-medication-soaked wad of hay. In addition, after you deposit the medicine in the horse's mouth, lift his chin up for 30 seconds or so to avoid a wad of paste dropping out onto the ground.

Fly Control

The first line of defence against flies is getting fresh manure away from the stables. (Manure management is probably the most important thing you can do for the health of your horse.) From there, you will need to deal with the flies themselves, using one of the many sprays or lotions that are on the market.

Using Fly Sprays

For years, I simply brought the spray bottle out to the paddock and sprayed the horses down each morning. At some point, after watching the spray settle on their hay and having it blow back into my face, I decided that this was not a good idea. Now, I reserve a brush especially for fly spray; I set the brush down, use the spray directly and then brush the horse. This method seems to avoid spray landing anywhere it wants, including in my lungs. You can also use a face mask.

Small biting flies of different varieties really like to get along the horse's stomach midline, in their ears, right at the top of their forelock and in other places the horse can't reach. Make sure you protect these places.

Never spray fly spray on the horse's face. Spray it on a glove or a small brush reserved exclusively for this purpose, and carefully apply it to the horse's face, avoiding his eyes.

Non-Chemical Methods of Fly Repellant

Garlic powder in the horse's feed is said to help control biting flies. It doesn't reduce the population per se, but at least the flies don't land. You can buy garlic powder or dried garlic chips by the tub specifically for this purpose. You will need to introduce it to your horse's feed gradually for a few weeks before the fly season starts. Garlic powder is also said to boost the immune system and enhance coat condition.

You can also buy mesh fly sheets that cover the horse's body but are light and not hot in warm weather. Another tactic is to put your horses in stables during the times of day when the flies are out in force – usually from midday to darkness – and leave them out overnight when the flies are not as bad.

Your Equine First Aid Kit

Don't wait for something to happen before you gather some basic first aid supplies. Having a first aid kit on hand can be the best insurance against having to use it. Know what is in the kit and what each item is for. As with all medications, make sure that your equine medicines are kept out of reach of pets and small children.

You can buy ready-made equine first aid kits in tack shops and from horse-supply catalogues. Although items can be less expensive when purchased singly, a first aid box provides a convenient way to keep everything together. Kits also often include a laminated information card about basic first aid. Once you have worked out what kinds of bandages and other supplies you like best, you can tailor your first aid kit to your own preferences.

If you assemble your own first aid kit, here are some items to include:

· Different kinds of bandages
· Gamgee
· Tube of antiseptic cream
· Antiseptic cleanser
· Hydrogen peroxide
· Vet wrap
· Rubber and/or latex gloves
· Thermometer, either digital or heavy-duty ring top with string attached
· Scissors
· Adhesive tape
· Hand wipes
· Arnica

In addition, keep a cold pack in the freezer for bruises and sprains. See Appendix A for a list of veterinary manuals.

Surface Wounds

You can clean these yourself with warm water and an antiseptic solution. If the wound is bleeding, bandage it if possible.

Deeper Lacerations

You should call your vet immediately for deeper lacerations, to determine the need for stitches. Puncture wounds need to be carefully examined to ascertain whether any part of the object is still lodged in the wound. Puncture wounds are exceptionally susceptible to infection, as dirt gets trapped and the airless environment provides a perfect breeding ground for bacteria. Your vet will be able to clean the wound, and will probably prescribe a precautionary course of antibiotics.

Hives

Hives show up as raised bumps, usually all over the horse's neck and body. In themselves, hives are not a serious issue and rarely even itch, although they look as though they should. However, they do indicate a reaction to something. Try to work out what has been introduced to your horse – a fly spray, a supplement – and avoid that product. Hives are common in the spring, when horses are losing their winter coats and new spring grass is coming through. Hives are usually treated with steroids.

What does proud flesh mean?
A wound that won't heal produces scar tissue that protrudes from the wound area. This scar tissue is commonly referred to as **proud flesh**.

Eye Wounds

One spring, my mare decided to give me a round of eye wounds to care for. I never found out what caused them, but one eye swelled up quite a bit. A month or two after the eye cleared up, she did it again, though less drastically. In both cases, the vet administered a green dye that allowed him to check for foreign objects in the eye. Then I had to administer a topical pupil-dilating ointment once a day for three days, as well as an antibiotic ointment twice a day for a week to ten days. I allowed her to go outside with a fly mask on to block the light, and she had full access to her stable so that she could get out of the sunlight if she chose. After a couple of days, she certainly hated to see me coming to poke ointment in her eye, but everything cleared up nicely both times. And she hasn't had an eye problem since.

General Health for the Geriatric Horse

It is to be hoped that your horse will be blessed with a long and healthy life. Horses commonly live to their late 20s and even over 30 these days. If your horse reaches that ripe old age, you can be proud of your equine management skills. By this age, the horse may be able to be ridden lightly – for instance, a little pony ride for your five-year-old nephew or a trip down the track and back each afternoon – but probably will no longer be rideable.

The ailment you are most likely to have to deal with is arthritis. With medication and/or support from natural products such as glucosamine, your elderly equine can probably be kept comfortable. For the arthritic horse, you need to be concerned with his ability to get up after lying down for a little nap or taking a little roll. If you stable your horses, give the older horse as large a stable as possible; some movement helps alleviate stiffness. If he is getting picked on or jostled around too much, you may find it necessary to separate him from the younger horses.

The other ailment you will most likely have to deal with is digestion. Old horses have worn teeth that just don't work the way they used to. Many commercial feeds are designed especially for senior equines. They are typically more palatable and are easier to chew. You may have to make an effort to keep enough weight on your horse.

Keep a close eye on your old friend, especially during winter months. Offer him a few extras – warmed water, a thicker rug – to help him live in comfortable retirement.

Of course, ultimately the older horse will present you with that heart-breaking decision of whether the time has come to have him put down. If you can keep him comfortable and enjoying life, that's great. But when the horse spends most of his day in noticeable pain and no longer cares about the world, it's time to be good to him. The unfortunate reality is that horses are large animals, and the disposal of their bodies is easier if it is preplanned. There are many options that you should discuss with your vet.

Prevention is Key

The things that can befall a horse are pretty overwhelming. Rectal prolapse, bowed tendons, scratches – the list is endless. Unless you have several horses for several years, the chance that you will experience even a small percentage of these is slim. The best expenditure of your time and money, and the best approach to benefit your horse, is in learning about how to keep horses in good health and practising good equine management and preventive measures.

CHAPTER 10

Beyond Conventional Health Care

E quine holistic practitioners – some of whom are also veterinarians – consider the whole patient and not just the disease, condition or symptoms. The goal is to understand the immediate problem and the contributing factors, and then to propose therapies that enable the horse to heal from within itself *and* prevent recurrences. Even in crisis situations such as colic and laminitis, when speedy veterinary attention is crucial, complementary therapies offer the horse owner additional strategies for better outcomes and recoveries, as well as preventative care. Holistic approaches are reviewed here in three categories: body work, nutritional support and energy work.

The Holistic Approach

Here are some suggestions for finding a holistic practitioner:

· Ask your vet or at local livery yards for recommendations.
· Check bulletin boards at tack shops, feed stores, health food stores, natural pharmacies and herb shops.
· Contact holistic veterinary organizations, such as the following, to find local practitioners:
  · British Association of Holistic Nutrition and Medicine, 8 Borough Court, Hartley Wintney, Basingstoke, Hampshire RG27 8JA; tel 01252 843282; *www.bahnm.org.uk*
  · British Association of Homeopathic Veterinary Surgeons, *www.bahvs.co.uk*
  · British Medical Acupuncture Society, The Administrator, BMAS House, 3 Winnington Court, Northwich, Cheshire CW8 1AQ; tel 01606 786782; *www.medical-acupuncture.co.uk*

What is alternative medicine?

Alternative medicine: this refers to diagnostic and treatment systems (modalities) not commonly taught in medical/veterinary schools, such as nutrition, herbal medicine, homeopathy, chiropractic and acutherapies.

Complementary medicine: this refers to natural treatments used in addition to conventional therapies, usually under the direction of a holistic vet and sometimes encouraged by traditional vets.

Holistic medicine: holistic approaches take into account a wide range of factors – all systems of the individual horse, as well as its care and overall environment – to propose preventative and treatment strategies to improve health and well-being.

Body Work

Massage

The muscular system of the horse accounts for 60 per cent of the horse's body weight and is entirely responsible for movement. It is also the seat of mobility problems, such as some lamenesses and reduced range of motion and flexibility, which can diminish performance. Whether your horse is a competitive athlete or accustomed to leisurely hacks, it's more than likely that at some point he'll experience muscle strain and spasms.

Always consult a veterinarian whenever your horse is ill or severely injured. If you're lucky enough to find a vet who knows and incorporates alternative methods, that is all the better for your horse.

Motion occurs solely because muscles move bones by contracting and folding over upon themselves. These folds then release so that the muscle can stretch to full length. Damaged, tight muscles cannot release completely. A muscle's ability to relax is reduced, and concussive stresses are transmitted down the line to other muscles and finally to the tendons, which have limited flexibility and are thus vulnerable to serious, sometimes permanent, damage. Because the horse often compensates for a damaged part by increasing stress on a healthy part, restrictions in one area of the body can appear somewhere else. Adding massage therapy to your routine before you exercise your horse will help him maintain supple muscles and efficient motion, and avoid tendon damage and torn tissue.

The basis of massage is to locate and relieve the tight muscle that leads to the muscle spasm that leads to restricted motion. If this is done early enough, further muscle damage can be avoided. Spasms are areas of clumped tendonous attachment tissue that cannot release.

If you are interested in massage and muscle release therapies for horses, find a practitioner in your area by contacting one of the following.

- Beth Darrall (Equine Bowen Therapy), 9 Byron Road, Cheltenham, Gloucestershire GL51 7HE; tel 01242 251465; *www.equinebowentherapy.com*
- Equine Sports Massage Association, St Georges Cottages, Brinkers Lane, Wadhurst, East Sussex TN5 6LT; tel 01892 785717; *www.equinemassageassociation.co.uk*

Chiropractic

Chiropractors focus on the relationship of the spinal column both to organic systems (nerves, organs and immune system) and to the biomechanics of movement. The key approach in chiropractic is manipulation, and the key to success is the skill and training of the person using the technique.

The laws of biomechanics require each part of the body to interact with others *precisely*. When one part in the equine body loses its specific relationship with its co-workers, thousands of kilograms of force can adversely affect the system. Long-term misalignments may be apparent in uneven muscle development or weight-bearing capacities. Even tiny structural changes can result in discomfort for the horse and will probably show up under saddle or in exercise.

Chiropractors use palpation – checking for pain or asymmetries with their hands – and flexion of the horse's limbs and joints to identify problem areas in the skeletal structure. Adjustments are made manually using a brief thrust at specific locations, or by manipulating the body of the horse to provide release in various joints. This should be a relatively gentle process, always without force.

For a chiropractor in your area, contact:

- McTimoney Chiropractic Association, 21 High Street, Eynsham, Oxfordshire OX29 4HE; tel 01865 880974; *www.mctimoney-chiropractic.org*

Acupressure

Acupressure is an easy and rewarding therapy that you can use yourself to protect, repair and promote the well-being of your horse. The benefits seem to be so vast and varied that you will probably want to devote more time than is possible here to learning the basic principles and developing your skills. Acupressure is based on the meridian system at the heart of traditional Chinese medicine (TCM). Meridians are pathways in the body along which flows the energy considered vital to health, known as *chi* (sometimes spelled *qi*). In TCM, it is thought that any block or break along a meridian causes a chi imbalance that may appear as illness or discomfort. The goal in TCM – and acupressure – is to maintain or repair interruptions in energy flow.

In TCM, the ear is considered a miniature representation of the entire body, making 'ear work' useful for relaxing a tense horse or rebalancing an injured or ill one. Ear work is also very relaxing for horses being shod or examined by a vet. Some basic ear massages involve gently rubbing the tips of the ears to help relax the horse, and rubbing in circles at the base of the ear to aid digestion and respiration. Make sure you gradually get your horse comfortable about having his ears touched before using this method for relieving stress.

The meridian system contains 12 main meridians, each related to major organ systems. Other points outside the 12 meridians are also important to the strong flow of chi. Zidonis, Soderberg and Snow's *Equine Acupressure: A Working Manual* is one good source for point location and provides a comprehensive overview and guidelines for using acupressure, including strategies for relieving many common problems.

Acupuncturists have used the Qi Gong Machine (QGM) in treatments for humans for years, and the device has now been proven very effective with horses. Equisonic QGM is designed specifically for horses. The machine emits low-level (infrasonic) sound waves in the 8–14hz range, at the opposite frequency range from ultrasound (20,000–100,000hz). Studies have shown that during hands-on healing, qi gong healers emit frequencies in this range. Because tissues do not heat up and there are no side effects, the QGMs can safely be used by anyone. It has helped horses recover from fractures, laminitis, chronic and acute inflammation, sprains, tendon damage, colic, puncture wounds and navicular disease.

The relationship between the acupoints and their effects may seem strange at first if you aren't used to Chinese therapies – the points used to relieve symptoms are often located at a distance from the apparent site of injury or illness. The spleen meridian, for example, which runs up the right hind leg and across the horse's barrel, is related to the immune system, the digestive tract and muscles and soft tissue. The first point on the spleen meridian (SP1), located on the right hind heel, is said to provide the horse's essential body energy. Stimulating SP1 balances the energy throughout the meridian. SP6 relieves gastrointestinal imbalances, including chronic diarrhoea; SP9 relieves stifle pain and enhances the immune system; and so on.

Basic acupressure is typically done by gently applying and releasing 0.9–1.8kg (2–4lb) of pressure with the thumb to stimulate points. Watch your horse as you work, to see whether you need to reduce pressure. He should relax, not tense, with your touch. Often the horse's lips, chin or eyelids will quiver as relief flows. He may yawn repeatedly. Work both the left and right sides of the horse from front to rear and top to bottom. Significant improvements are often immediately apparent, making acupressure a valuable adjunct to other therapies, improving recovery time and outcomes.

Herbs and Nutritional Supplements

Herbs for Health

Herbal medicine was a primary base of veterinary care until the 20th century. Today, many pharmaceutical drugs are based on natural and synthetic versions of the active compounds in plants. However, there is more value to herbs than just their active chemical compounds, and often much benefit is lost in the process of isolating active ingredients for the pharmaceutical version. According to Dr Andrew Weil, a well-known proponent of natural medicine in the USA, plant-based drugs can be more toxic than the natural form of the plant.

It is rare for horses today to have access to the range of plants their ancestors encountered in the wild or in country pastures, but if they do, they will instinctively select the botanicals that contain what they need. In her book, *A Modern Horse Herbal*, herbalist Hilary Page Self says, 'Normally, unless forced by starvation, [horses] will not voluntarily eat any fodder which will do them harm. Therefore be aware of this and be guided by it. If the horse is not enthusiastic about a particular herb, find an alternative one to feed.' She also says that horses will refuse a herb they've readily accepted once they no longer require its support.

Medicinal herbs can enhance conventional medical treatment, boost and support the immune system for preventative maintenance, and offer remedies for some common problems that plague horses and the humans who care for them. Most remedies are based on repeated observation of the choices made by animals in a natural environment when they are ill or injured.

Herbs can be added to the horse's feed, used as simple topical remedies or as poultices for swellings, bites or abscesses. As in other aspects of horse care, it's possible to spend a lifetime studying herbs and not have enough time to learn half of everything there is to know. However, there are great resources available from people who *have* studied extensively, which you can use as references if you decide to add natural herbal support to your horse care routine.

More and more health food stores and speciality shops offer a wide array of botanical options. A 450kg (1,000lb) horse requires about 30g (1oz) of the herb of choice a day, so it pays to find out whether you can get mail-order discounts for bulk purchases. There are also companies that specialize in providing herbal blends that have already been combined for use in specific circumstances.

There are herbal answers to a wide range of questions about equine health. It's important to educate yourself or to find a knowledgeable source to be sure you're helping your horse, not creating problems. Not all herbs are safe for long-term use or for every situation. Also, remember that many drugs are based on botanicals, and some herbs will show up as banned substances in competition drug tests.

Dried herbs are simple to store. Cold does them no harm, so you can keep them at the stables during the winter. Avoid direct sunlight and damp areas – a dry, dark place is best. Store them in a container with a tight-fitting lid, such as a glass jar.

Garlic

Dozens of recent studies have shown that ancient garlic-eaters, such as the Egyptians, were on to something important. Garlic has been shown to lower human blood cholesterol and blood pressure and prevent heavy metal poisoning. It can even slow the growth of certain tumours. It is also commonly fed to horses as an insect repellent. Horses excrete the sulphur from garlic through their skin, which keeps insects away.

However, one of the most important uses for garlic with equines is colic prevention. Garlic supports the good bacteria so vital to digestion. Since antibiotics wipe out all bacteria, feeding garlic is valuable after conventional antibiotics have been given, to encourage the good bacteria to re-establish. Garlic also acts as an antibiotic, and has been particularly effective with respiratory infections and for seasonal respiratory allergies such as hay fever. It can prevent wounds from becoming infected by stimulating the production of white blood cells to strengthen general resistance to infection and improve the immune system. Louis Pasteur, who developed pasteurization, thought garlic was just as effective in some situations. It's powerful stuff – and powerfully smelly, too – but nothing worthwhile comes without some sort of price!

Garlic can be fed raw if your horse will eat it (some won't, others love it) or in powdered or dried forms (cold-processed to retain the key ingredients). Add it to your horse's feed gradually over the course of a week to get her accustomed to the strong flavour. A 450kg (1,000lb) horse can be given 4–5 large or 6–8 small crushed cloves a day, or 15–30g (1/2–1oz) of powder or granules. (Make sure you seal the lid tightly on powdered garlic to prevent it from clumping in humid weather.)

If you are giving garlic for general well-being, add the garlic to feed for about six weeks or so and then reduce and eliminate the dose. Herbalist Hilary Page Self recommends that herbs be used not on a year-round basis, but with occasional breaks in order to give the body the chance to take over on its own. If your horse seems to be at his best with garlic, resume using the herb after a break. Start adding garlic a couple of weeks before the season starts if your horse has allergies or if you use it to deter insects, and keep her on it throughout the period that gives her trouble.

Rosehips

The high concentration of vitamin C in rosehips is great for fighting infection and helping to restore health after a long illness. Botanical sources of nutrients provide the additional benefits, such as fibre, that supplements don't, making rosehips a good choice over a vitamin C supplement. In *A Modern Horse Herbal*, Hilary Page Self reports that she has found rosehips extremely effective in promoting strong, healthy hooves. Feed 15g (¹/₂oz) of chopped rosehip shells a day.

Dandelions are a rich source of vitamins A, B, C and D, and minerals such as potassium, magnesium and calcium. They are effective for liver or kidney disorders. Collect fresh dandelion leaves at any time during the season. Dig for roots in mid to late summer to get the best benefits. (Avoid collecting dandelions from lawns treated with chemicals, though.)

Slippery Elm

The powdered bark from the slippery elm tree can be used as a poultice to encourage wounds to heal (mix the powder with boiling water and let it cool to encourage it to stick before you bandage). It helps internally, too, for digestive problems, including ulcers, and is typically gentle enough for even sensitive horses. Add 2 tablespoons to plain yoghurt or honey, and add it to the feed.

Nutritional Supplements

Humans are discovering the benefits of adding a wide range of supplements to their diets to support good health. The fact is that even if you eat organically grown foods, you might not be able to consume enough to meet your body's requirements for the nutrients that cells need. If the majority of the food you eat is commercially grown, the evidence is that modern farming techniques, based largely on synthetic fertilizers and single-crop fields, have stripped much of the mineral content from the soil and thus from the foods we eat. Processing also destroys many vital nutrients.

The same is true for horse feeds. As mentioned before, horses have much more limited access to the wide variety of grasses and plants in the wild that would supply their needs. So what's an owner to do? Select the best food you can find, and consider bridging the nutritional gap with specific supplements. The following are a few that have found their way into feed rooms around the world.

Antioxidants

When you leave iron tools out in the weather, they oxidize, which produces rust. A similar degenerative process happens in cells. In the metabolic process, the body produces oxides, which are known as free radicals. Antioxidants are key components in the free radical defence system. (Familiar examples of antioxidants are vitamins A, C and E.) When all is going well, the balance between free radicals and antioxidants keeps cellular damage manageable. However, in times of illness and other stresses – including exposure to pollution, heavy metals and chemicals – free radicals can overwhelm the body's immune system, leaving the horse vulnerable to infections and illness, perhaps even cancer. Supplemental antioxidants can help return stressed horses to health or prevent stress exposure from negatively impacting health. The body will use and store only the antioxidants it requires, eliminating excess levels. Ideally, your veterinarian can help you determine the best strategy for supplementation.

MSM

MSM (methylsulphonylmethane) is an organic sulphur used by the body to produce enzymes for digestion and antibodies to fight infection and to build connective tissue (for example, cartilage, skin and hooves). MSM, used in conjunction with glucosamine, is often recommended for arthritic symptoms to rebuild the cartilage that cushions the bones. It also supports the body to reduce allergic reactions. If your horse gets hives, MSM can erase this allergic reaction.

Glucosamine

Osteoarthritis seems to go hand in hand with an athletic life. When the cartilage that lines the joints to keep bones from rubbing together deteriorates because of wear and tear or age, crippling pain can result. An arthritic horse may be stiff before warming up or may resist work that used to be easy for him. Arthritis was once considered incurable, but with the discovery of nutritional supports such as glucosamine and MSM, the effects of this degenerative disease can be arrested, if not reversed.

Glucosamine can actually rebuild damaged cartilage, in contrast to anti-inflammatory drugs, which mask the pain and therefore can speed up the process of deterioration from overuse. If you and your veterinarian suspect arthritis (if your horse has ever taken a fall, broken a bone or is in his teens, it's likely), try glucosamine, additional vitamin C and MSM. (It is worth noting that there is evidence that glucosamine HC1 is more absorbable than glucosamine sulphate.)

You should see a change in about a month. If it's effective, you can keep your horse on glucosamine for the rest of his life; this is a substance that the body produces naturally, and there are no known side effects from this kind of supplementation. It costs about 50p–£1 a day to free your horse from arthritis pain. The supplier will provide the right dosage frequency and amounts based on your horse's weight.

Probiotics

Your horse's digestive health may be your primary concern as an owner. Colic is the number one killer of horses, and anything we can do to keep our horses from getting colic is worth knowing about.

Horses process feed with the aid of various digestive bacteria (intestinal flora). These friendly bacteria are greatly reduced in number when your horse is under antibiotic treatment or under stress caused by long-distance travelling, loss of a companion, a move to a new home and so on. Also, if you change feed (which should always be done slowly), new flora must develop to break down the new feed. Adding beneficial bacteria (probiotics) to your horse's diet can help him recover more quickly from an illness or difficult adjustment and reduce the chances of colic.

Horse-specific probiotics are widely available from feed stores and by mail order, and dosage suggestions come on the package. Older horses or those prone to mild colic episodes may especially benefit from probiotics. In a pinch, you can use acidophilus, made for humans, which is available at health food stores or pharmacies. Empty three to five capsules into some apple sauce, mix and add to the feed twice a day for about two weeks. Your horse will eat it up, and the helpful bacteria will help him digest his food efficiently.

The list of dietary supplements is extensive, and as you become more involved with horses, you will find that you add them based on your horse's health and needs. You certainly won't need them all, and you may not need any if your horse is thriving and energetic. But we all age; as time passes, the body can't make or absorb some nutrients as efficiently. Of course, as with anything, we can get carried away with tubs of supplements and generate quite a brew to prepare at the horse's mealtimes. But used wisely, nutritional supplements could add useful years to your horse's life.

If your horse's hives are unusually severe or haven't gone in a day or so, or if they get worse, call your vet immediately. Allergic reactions can be serious.

Energy Therapies

For thousands of years, Asian cultures have perfected techniques to improve the flow of life energy called *chi*. Energy practitioners enhance energy to improve total health through various remedies (homeopathics or Bach flower remedies), tools (needles, magnets, sonic devices or lasers), or their hands, as with Reiki.

Acupuncture

Acupuncturists use extremely fine needles to release areas of blocked *chi* at specific acupoints along the meridians, as discussed in the acupressure section. Once normal energy flow is re-established, circulation of *chi* increases to stimulate the nervous system to restore normal function in a body system that was depleted. Another benefit of acupuncture is the release of endorphins, the body's own 'feelgood' chemicals. As a result of these benefits, horses generally find acupuncture quite soothing.

Acupuncture is often the treatment of choice for performance problems linked to skeletal issues (such as navicular disease, disc problems, arthritis and inflamed joints). It has also proven effective for conditions such as allergies, nerve injuries, reproductive disorders, COPD, kidney failure and liver ailments.

Acupuncturists palpate the acupoints to make diagnoses and determine the best treatment. Many more vets are training in this ancient medical art, so it won't be impossible to find someone; if your vet isn't licensed for acupuncture, perhaps he or she can refer you to someone.

Homeopathy

Homeopathic remedies are gaining in popularity, both with horse people and veterinarians. Homeopathy has been practised for about 200 years in Europe and the United States. In Britain it is illegal for anyone other than a Royal College of Veterinary Surgeons-registered vet to prescribe treatments, although owners may treat their own horses. The basic premise of homeopathic medicine is that 'like cures like', a theory first proposed by Hippocrates, the father of medicine. A substance that in large doses would produce symptoms can, in tiny doses, alleviate those symptoms. Homeopathic remedies stimulate the body's defence system to cope with the problem in a way similar to that in which vaccines operate.

The natural animal, vegetable or mineral substance that a homeopathic remedy is based on is present only at an electromagnetic level, which makes this branch of natural medicine difficult to understand, although its effectiveness has been proven over and over.

Homeopathic practitioners use individual symptoms and case studies to devise a strategy to treat chronic or complex problems. Success may depend on the experience the practitioner has in prescribing remedies, so work with a vet or practitioner who has formally studied this art for the best chances of success. However, simple conditions may be treated at home with specific remedies that are generally available through vitamin suppliers, pharmacies or health food stores.

New uses for laser therapy are being discovered all the time. The modern low-level laser has become an important adjunct to acutherapies. Also, owners can safely use lasers on acupoints or to effectively stimulate the body to fight off infection, which can be especially helpful if the horse has a reaction to antibiotics or other medications, or you need quick results and can't wait for herbs to take effect. One caution: never shine a laser directly into the eye.

To administer a homeopathic remedy, insert four to six pellets or tablets (based on your horse's weight) into an apple (carve a little hole in it) or dissolve them in a little water and squirt the liquid onto his tongue. Be careful not to touch the remedy with your hands, as this will reduce its potency. You can also add the pellets or tablets to feed if your horse is suspicious of medications in general, although horses can carefully eat all of the grain in their bucket and leave the remedy behind if they desire. Only use the remedy until the symptoms are relieved, and use only one type at a time. Store them in a dark, cool, dry place.

Here are some remedies you should have on hand to treat trauma:

· **Arnica montana:** everyone should have arnica on hand. It can practically erase bruising and inflammation after an injury such as a kick, fall or sprain. It also treats or prevents shock in cases of colic or other trauma. It's superior to bute for relieving swelling, tendon strain or muscle pain after a workout. Many riders keep it on hand for their own use as well! Use 30X or 30C potency immediately after an accident, one dose every 15 minutes for an hour or so, then a dose every five hours, reduced to a dose every 12 hours until the pain and swelling have gone. Arnica gel is effective applied externally for swelling or bruising.

· **Rhus tox:** use Rhus tox for sprains, tendons or ligament injuries. Start with arnica, then change when the pain and swelling have reduced. Give one dose every morning until improvement is apparent.

· **Ruta graveolens:** this remedy is particularly effective for tendons, ligaments and joints. Start with a course of arnica and then change to a dose of Ruta graveolens once or twice a day.

· **Aconite:** use for sudden stress, shock or panic, such as that caused by injury or colic. Dose hourly for up to four hours.

Keep the following remedies on hand to treat allergies:

· **Apis mellifica, Antimonium crudum and Urtica urens:** use for hives or other soft, fluid-filled swellings, such as insect bites. Apis is also good for filled tendons. Dose hourly until swelling subsides. If you don't see results overnight or symptoms increase, call your vet – a severe allergic reaction may be occurring.

· **Mixed pollens and Arundo:** Use for summer airborne pollens if your horse is shaking his head or has a runny nose from seasonal allergies. One dose up to three times a day can give relief.

Here are some remedies useful for treating wounds:

· **Ledum:** Ledum is very effective for puncture wounds. Administer three or four times daily.

· **Hypericum:** Hypericum is good for punctures, muscle spasms and after surgery. Administer three times a day.

Bach Flower Remedies

Bach Flower remedies can be thought of as homeopathy for the emotions. Dr Edward Bach developed flower remedies in the 1930s to help human patients restore the harmony between mind and body necessary for the well-being of each. Today, many holistic animal practitioners swear by the power of Bach Flower remedies to help horses (and every other animal, not to mention humans) to reduce or eliminate negative emotions so that they can cope better with stressful activities or events. If your horse is traumatized, anxious, nervous or fearful, Bach Flower essences can be used alone or as an appropriate complement to alternative and conventional treatments.

The power of these remedies comes primarily from flowers, although other botanicals and even minerals may be the basis for remedies. They work not on the cellular system but on the subtle energies of the body. They have no side effects; if you use an inappropriate remedy, it simply has no effect. There are 38 individual remedies, plus the combination remedy known as Rescue Remedy. With the assistance of brochures available where you purchase the flower essences, select the appropriate remedy based on your horse's personality and behaviour. For example, walnut is useful in helping horses cope with changing circumstances, such as when moving to a new home.

Rescue Remedy is the most famous of the Bach Flower remedies. It contains a blend of five flower essences specific to reducing the effects of trauma and shock. If your horse suffers the loss of a stable mate, or has an accident or illness, this remedy can reverse shock (both physical and emotional) and panic. (This remedy is good for people, too.)

To use remedies, put four drops on a sugar cube or carrot and feed it to the horse. You can also add about ten drops of one or two remedies to a small amount of water (spring water is best) in a spray bottle and spray it around the horse's shoulders, neck and face. Another option is to spray your palm and cup it lightly over his nostril for a few breaths, and then rub the rest on his muzzle. Remedies can also be added to feed. Rescue Remedy's calming effects can help in an emergency situation.

Magnetic Therapy

Magnets have been used in health care for centuries to improve circulation, oxygen absorption and cell function. The theory is that the iron atoms in blood corpuscles respond to magnetism to enhance blood flow, which aids in the elimination of waste products and in cellular regeneration. A similar action is thought to carry calcium ions to broken bones. Studies on horses have shown increased blood flow and improved soft tissue function and bone health in the majority of horses tested. Magnetic therapy has been used effectively to treat fractures, wounds, joint problems and sprains non-invasively.

Magnetic fields are created by the flow of energy between a north and a south pole in static magnets (think of the magnets that hold your shopping list on the fridge). Magnetic therapy leg wraps, hoof wraps and rugs have been developed for equine uses.

By following a few basic rules, magnets can safely be used by anyone. (As always in cases of serious injury or illness, call in a professional for evaluation and treatment recommendations.) Magnets should only be used for a few consecutive hours or, under vet supervision, a few days at a time. Equine product manufacturers recommend that you don't use magnets on open wounds or burns, on injuries that are less than 48 hours old or are hot, or over liniments or chemicals such as fly sprays.

Magnetic therapy has been used to improve laminitis outcomes, heal abscesses, relieve inflamed hocks, improve hoof growth and heal soft tissue injuries, as well as to help muscles remain supple after a hard workout and keep muscles warm between competitive events. This gentle therapy may very well help a horse with a chronic condition such as inflammation or poor hoof health to regain a level of soundness.

TTouch

The Tellington Touch (TTouch) was developed by Linda Tellington-Jones Kleger from work she did with Moshe Feldenkrais in the 1970s. Feldenkrais developed a system of gentle, non-habitual movements and manipulations (the Feldenkrais Method of Functional

Integration) to redirect human body patterns that had been established in response to dysfunction, tension or pain. These new patterns of movement were said to awaken unused brain cells and establish new neural pathways. People from all over the world used the Feldenkrais Method and found relief from pain and new freedom of movement. Some even recovered from paralysis. With TTouch, the primary goal is to enhance the health, performance and well-being of the horse, as well as to foster communication and trust between horse and handler. It is recommended that the owner or primary handler of the horse be the one to use TTouch on the horse, to increase the connection between them.

Here are the four basic TTouch techniques:

1. Stroking with your flat hand to increase circulation and calm the horse.
2. Cupping the hand and using the fingertips to move the horse's skin in small or large circles of one and a quarter revolutions.
3. Cupping the hands and patting the horse over the entire body to stimulate blood circulation.
4. Taking up a roll of skin between the thumbs and fingers and sliding it along the muscle surface in straight lines.

TTouch for horses incorporates stretches, mouth work, tail work and ear work to release tension and increase the horse's sense of security. TTouch is often part of a programme that includes ground exercises and bodywork called TTEAM (The Tellington-Touch Equine Awareness Method). These techniques promise to increase willingness, horse-human rapport and athletic performance. Tellington-Jones Kleger also has a riding component based on her 30 years of experience.

Learn about TTouch techniques from Linda Tellington-Jones Kleger's books (see Appendix A), videos and clinics – contact UK TTEAM Centre, Tilley Farm, Farmborough, Bath, Somerset BA2 0AB; tel 01761 471182; *www.tilleyfarm.co.uk*. You can also check out the original website at *www.tellingtontouch.com*.

Reiki

Reiki is a gentle therapy used on people to improve recovery rates after surgery as well as to treat physical problems. It can be used in the same way on horses. Using their hands, Reiki practitioners boost the body's own energy flow to open pathways where *chi* may be blocked. Once students have been attuned by a Reiki master, they find that they can sense areas where energy is blocked; these areas feel warmer than surrounding areas, in response to the greater draw of energy there. Hands-on energy work requires no diagnosis, because the body will simply take the energy it needs from Reiki treatments to re-establish healthy *chi* movement throughout the body. As internal energy resumes its vital flow, healing can begin.

If you get the chance to watch a Reiki session, do so. Generally, a treatment lasts 40–60 minutes, depending on the horse's needs. Reiki soothes emotional unrest as well as helping a horse recover from physical illness or injury. The response from a horse as the energy pathways open can be dramatic. The eyes close and the head drops. The horse may yawn or work its mouth. The breathing deepens and often gut sounds increase (making Reiki useful in treating the early stages of colic). The horse's entire body reflects the deep level of relaxation taking place, usually within 10–15 minutes. Some horses even fall asleep.

Reiki won't replace your veterinarian, who you should always call immediately in an emergency, but it could make a tremendous difference in your horse's recovery in an emergency or chronic situation, for example when you are waiting for the vet to treat a colicky horse. It can help to minimize sprains and strains (especially in conjunction with homeopathics and cold hosing or ice), maintain chiropractic adjustments, soothe sore feet – the list goes on.

The best thing about Reiki is that anyone can do it. In about a day, a Reiki master can give Reiki to you, your horses and your pets. Reiki givers also receive energy when giving it, making Reiki an all-round win-win situation.

Take Control With Alternative Therapies

As you can see, alternative therapies often give horse owners some ability to help their horses in chronic and acute situations, and they definitely increase comfort for the horse. While you probably won't be using all of these techniques, you may find a few particularly helpful, depending on your situation. While I can't emphasize enough that these treatments do not take the place of your regular veterinarian, they might help you see your veterinarian a little less often! Of course, you should always let your vet know what you have been doing on your own, and seek his or her advice, and do the same with a licensed practitioner of any therapy when you are unsure or just learning.

CHAPTER 11

Handling

When it comes to horses, handling is every-thing. Your safety, and often the horse's safety depends on your understanding of the best ways to handle your horse. The basics of handling revolve around something known as groundwork – that is, working with and educating your horse on the ground, as opposed to in the saddle. Much of what good groundwork consists of will clearly translate into things that are also useful when riding your horse.

Why is Good Handling Important?

As you learned in Chapter 4, the horse's world revolves around the need for order, and understanding his place in that order. *Where* he is in that pecking order isn't the important thing to your horse, but *knowing where he is* on that ladder is important to his peace of mind. So if you and your horse are attached by a lead rope and he decides you aren't running the show, he will put himself in charge – and he will lead you. I suspect it won't take long before you become concerned that your horse's decisions often aren't in your best interests, or his.

I've been to many clinics where handling practices are taught, and have seen many a horse – both young and old – lead her handler into the arena or round pen to begin their lesson. It's a sorry sight and an unsafe situation as well, but it's encouraging to see that the owner has decided it's best to learn a new way of being with his or her horse.

What does conditioned response mean?
Conditioned response is a training approach in which a horse (or any thinking animal, including humans) is conditioned to respond to the same stimulus the same way every time she confronts that stimulus.

It is definitely the person on the end of the lead rope who can make a difference; the same horse in the hands of two different people acts very differently. When I decided to get back into horses again and bought my two-year-old gelding, he dragged me around all summer. I worked hard to establish my leadership role, but what I was offering wasn't sufficient for him. However, the person I bought him from could handle him much better than I could. The handler was clearly the factor. Although it was quite frustrating at the time, I look back and am really glad that this horse gave me a clear reason for wanting to find a way to interact safely with horses, and to attempt to become the kind of person that a horse could look to for support.

Why the Left Side?

Many myths surround why it is traditional for most of what we do with the horse to be done from the left side. The most logical one comes from the need to mount on the left because of the position of the soldier's sword in battle. Well, most of us aren't using our horses in battle or carrying swords when we ride, so forget this 'left side only' nonsense! The idea that this is some hard and fast rule has created many one-sided horses.

Yes, you'll find most halters and bridles do up on the left, but you could alter them to operate from the right. Even if you don't go to that extreme, it pays to be mindful of working both sides of your horse. A good handler who wants to build a solid, reliable horse will make sure that his or her horse is as 'two-sided' as possible, exposing it to new things from both sides and not doing everything from the traditional left. You could, for example, put the saddle pad on and gird up on the right side.

Interestingly, horses are often more pushy on the left side than they are on the right. That's because the left is where they are usually handled the most and where they have learned to be able to push their human handler around.

Handling the Young Foal

Good handling needs to start the first time a human comes into contact with a foal. This doesn't mean you need to halter a three-day-old filly and drill her with groundwork exercises for two-hour stints. That is definitely not a good idea. But what it does mean is that every time the human interacts with that filly – halter on or not – that interaction needs to be handling that is conducive to desirable behaviour.

No matter what the foal's age, it does not need to step on you, knock you out of the way or otherwise consider you something not to be considered. Each simple interaction can teach the foal to be yielding and step away from your pressure, not resist, brace against it or move into it. One touch and one step is the first building block, negative or positive. Even simply scratching the young horse can be not only an enjoyable experience but also an educational one. By continuing to scratch only

when the foal is behaving himself and moving him away (very important –
don't let him move *you* away!) when he is being obnoxious about it
teaches him that only respectful behaviour gets respectful and generous
behaviour in return.

Clicker training is a popular dog-training method that has become popular
in the horse world. It involves repeatedly asking for a specific action,
rewarding the performance of that action with a treat, and marking the
desired action with a click from a little clicker box or even a click of your
tongue. The click is then used to recall and reinforce that action. There are
books, videos and clinics that demonstrate the correct method of doing
this type of conditional-response training.

Although a very young foal usually does not need to be led (she will follow
her mother anywhere), if you do need to lead her, run the lead rope
around her rump to help encourage forward movement and avoid setting
up a pulling match. You might as well avoid pulling matches with horses,
because even a foal will win.

These are tiny steps taken over the six months or so that the foal is
suckling. Once she has been weaned and is more independent, it is
time to take all the steps you've set up since birth and begin to build
on them. Again, this doesn't mean taking a young horse and training
him and drilling him for hours each day. Let the horse be a horse for a
while – once he is under saddle, he will spend the rest of his life
working for you. So having the first two or three years to just play
seems like a fair deal.

Groundwork in Earnest

There are a couple of things that I have found to be the keys to being able to
safely manoeuvre a horse on the end of a lead rope.

Keeping Their Distance

Beginners are usually taught to lead their horse by standing to the horse's left and holding the lead rope right at the clip, where it attaches to the horse's halter. I have come to believe that this is dangerous. First, this tight grip on the horse is just one more way in which we confine this large animal and satisfy our own need to restrict his movement. Second, if the horse does spook at something from the right side, he has nowhere to go but on top of the handler – he can't jump forwards because his forward movement is blocked by the tight hold on the lead rope.

What is groundwork?
Groundwork is teaching your horse at the end of a lead rope. Many of the things you teach him in groundwork are transferable to the saddle.

Give the horse his own space. Teach your horses to lead 30–60cm (1–2ft) behind you – you can walk either directly in front or to one side or the other. If the horse spooks from either side, he can jump without jumping on you. If he spooks forwards, the freedom you are giving his head allows him to jump ahead to either side of you, which is what he will choose to do – if you've taught him that running you over is unacceptable under any circumstances.

If you don't want your horse to run over you, you must first earn his respect. In the wild herd, the horses on the lower rungs of the pecking order would never dream of pummelling a higher-ranking individual. But some domesticated horses are more bold than others and look to challenge the pecking order status quo. You need to show these individuals more presence than you might need to show others. If your horse doesn't tend to challenge your position as leader, you can probably just send some energy up the length of the lead rope when he comes closer than you want. Don't keep henpecking him, though; send just enough energy up the lead rope to match his eagerness. He will soon learn the rules of appropriate distance.

With the more bold horse, you will need to do what it takes for him to understand that you mean what you say. In the words of Ray Hunt, author of *Think Harmony with Horses*, 'Do as much or as little as it takes to get the change you are looking for.' This doesn't mean you should beat your horse (this isn't about submission but about leadership and safety), but it may mean a bop on the end of the nose with the lead rope (or more!) for the more bold horse. If your car is on the line when you see a train coming, you will step on the pedal as hard as it takes to get that car off the line in time to avoid that train, I imagine. If your horse learns to run you over, that bop on the nose or whack with a jacket or whatever you choose will seem pretty mild compared to hoof tracks up your back.

If you feel bad about this, then think about how little good you would be to him when you're in the hospital recovering. If you get the horse as a youngster, you can teach him enough about respect so this won't happen to begin with. If you are trying to change behaviour taught to the horse by other people, the more effective you are, the quicker the change will happen and you can both be happier.

Moving the Hindquarters

This is perhaps the single most useful move your horse could know. The goal is to have your horse learn that if you turn her head to the right and add some energy with your hand, arm or the end of the lead rope (or eventually your mind), she is to put her right hind foot underneath her in front of the left hind foot, and move her whole hindquarters to her left – and vice versa for the left. This move not only expands your horse's bend and flexibility, but also makes it possible, for example, to bring your horse out of a paddock full of other horses clamouring to get out, or to bring her into her stable and turn her to face you while you latch the stable door – the list of places where this moves comes in handy is endless. And as with all other groundwork you do, this move is pretty useful when you are riding as well!

Yielding to Pressure

Your horse should understand to yield to pressure, not brace against it or fight it. When your horse thoroughly understands this, you should be able to simply place your hand on her side with meaning to get her to move away from it. If she accidentally steps on her lead rope and pulls on her head, she will back up away from the pressure and free the lead rope, rather than fighting against it and ripping it out from under her foot.

The only time it is safe to tie your horse is after she gains a thorough understanding of yielding to pressure. Understanding how to yield to pressure will also be helpful if she gets caught in fence wire, for example; there is a much better chance that she will not struggle and really hurt herself, but instead wait to be released. Yielding to pressure means that when you go to put your horse's halter on, she will drop her head and help you get it in the right place, not throw her head up as high as she can and make it more difficult. If you need to back her up one step, you can ask for one step; when you get it and release the pressure, one step is all she'll move. True yielding is not a conditioned-response thing; it really means something to the horse.

Never learning to brace against pressure, but yielding instead gives your horse a frame of reference that will make her so enjoyable and safe to be around that you will find it difficult to understand why everyone doesn't want their horses to operate in this way.

Confinement

Humans seem to spend a lot of time concocting ways to confine horses – stables, paddocks, halters, bridles, bits, side reins – the list is endless, and it is being expanded and refined all the time. Below are the two best things you can do for your horse from the beginning of your time together, whether you are raising a foal or starting with a horse of any age:

1. Consider his mental fitness as much as his physical fitness. A horse with a calm mind will be able to listen to you and learn from you. I believe many people concentrate on fussing over a horse's body because it is more accessible and therefore a little easier to work out. If you don't understand the horse's mind, then I hope what is in this book can inspire you to find some good help in increasing your understanding.

2. Develop a mutually respectful relationship that allows you to trust your horse enough to give her some space. If the horse has to be on the end of a lead rope, then at least she can have 60–90cm (2–3ft) of rope instead of being gripped at the clip. Many people can't give their horses that much space, because the horse will constantly be diving for grass or prancing around. This is where it is your job to teach the horse that dragging you around the front lawn is simply unacceptable. I suspect most people with children are pretty quick to teach their kids that dragging mummy by the hand through the supermarket to the sweets aisle is not the way they want them to behave. Why they don't want their horses to learn a similar lesson about respectful behaviour is a mystery to me!

So give your horse a better life by teaching her to be respectful, which in turn allows you to trust her, which in turn allows you to stop trying to confine her so much. A horse who knows she can move if she absolutely has to is more likely to be OK about standing still when you want her to. Once you learn enough to not be so intent on confining your horse, you will breathe a sigh of relief – and so will your horses!

Everyday Handling

Entering a Stable

The two main issues that come up with entering a stable are the horse who does not want to be caught and the horse who mauls you when you enter with his meal. Both of these situations are the result of small incidents that build up into safety concerns. Be aware of the small incidents, and don't let them get any further than that.

Bringing Breakfast

To teach your horse to be respectful of you when you enter his stable with his feed, you need to have a picture in mind of what you would like your horse to look like when you enter. I suspect most of us would be content for our horses to stand back from the door, face us and wait patiently for us to put down feed bucket and fill the hay rack.

First, keep in mind that this can be a lot to ask of a horse in the domestic environment. We confine horses to a space not much bigger than their bodies, sometimes for extraordinary periods of time. Then we regulate their eating, a process totally opposite of their wild instincts of roaming and grazing 24 hours a day. No wonder they are a little anxious when we arrive with their meal!

The twitch has long been a means of restraint for the horse. By squeezing the thick layer of skin on the end of the horse's nose with a twitch, you are giving the horse something else to think about besides that wormer or other medication you are trying to administer. The twitch is used in an area known to be an acupressure point, one that releases natural pain-relieving, soothing endorphins that help the horse relax in general.

The Benefit of Respect

As mentioned earlier, if you spend as much time working with your horse's mental being as with his physical being, you will be one step ahead of the game. Your horse may still be anxious to get his grub, but teaching him a respectful way to act when you walk in the stable will make life a bit easier. The basic premise is not to enter the stable with the horse's food until he is a living example of that picture you have in your mind of him standing away from the door, facing you. It may take a couple of weeks to teach the generally respectful horse. The less respectful, more bold horse may take a little more encouragement for that ideal picture to shape up. You may need to physically ask her to back away from the door by placing your hands on her and asking her to step away from your pressure. For a very assertive horse, you may need to halter her before bringing her food in, and then ask her to back away from the door. Do only what it takes to get the picture you want – don't do too much and risk frightening the horse.

Feeding a horse treats by hand is perhaps fun for the human, but few people are capable of feeding a horse by hand without setting up obnoxious and pushy behaviour in an animal with a very powerful jaw and head. If you want to feed your horse treats, put them in her food bucket.

Catching Your Horse

In the Stable

If your horse turns his head into a corner and his rear end to you when you want to catch him in his stable, you have allowed something to shape up here that can be very dangerous. You need to be experienced enough to know the fine line between what is enough to get a change and what is too much for the horse. If things have got this far, get that trusted and experienced friend to help you. Your intention is to change the horse's mind about which direction he wants to face, and you definitely do not want to frighten the horse.

A horse who is afraid of you entering her stable can put you in a very dangerous situation, and you can easily make it worse. In fact, you can turn this into a vicious circle – the horse turns its rump to you when you enter its stable, so you feel the need to do something about it. But if you do too much, the horse will react even more defensively (he may kick out). Remember, although horses can find their stable to be a place of comfort, they can also feel very trapped. Their natural instinct to flee is not available to them in any way. The next instinct – to defend themselves – is the only thing they have. If sufficiently threatened (remember, 'sufficiently' is different for each horse), they will position themselves to kick you or, less likely but still possible, lunge at you with teeth bared. Either event is unpleasant at best, for you and for your horse.

When you and your experienced friend work with this horse, the object is to get the horse to turn to face you. Your horse should be ready and willing to be haltered when you enter the stable, and this is what you are trying to teach him. Do not expect the horse to turn and face you all at once. Look for small signs that he is making an attempt to work out what you want and that he feels OK about doing it. Look for an ear to turn in your direction, or even for him to simply turn his head but not his body. Step away from the horse the minute you get any sign he is becoming willing. By taking the pressure off him, you will give your horse the signal that his reaction is right and that you are giving him the physical and mental space he needs to make the turn.

Outside the Stable

The horse who is turning her rear to you in the stable is having the same problem as the horse that can't be caught in the pasture, only the size of the space is different. The pasture is probably less dangerous for you (although people have a remarkable ability to get themselves in danger with horses), since the horse has a place to go to get away from you and doesn't have to be so defensive. But all that space will be exhausting and perhaps make it frustrating and make you angry – which is never a good thing with horses.

> Don't get too cocky about your relationship with your horse – all horses will have days when kicking up their heels with their friends will seem a better idea than anything you have in mind! But if you have built a solid relationship, you will find this more entertaining than frustrating.

The horse who respects you and considers you supremely important (a tall order, but a good one to work towards) will give you her attention when you step into her space – paddock, pasture or stable. She has learned that being with you is a pretty good place to be, maybe even as good as being with her mates. A horse with which you have built this kind of relationship will position herself to be caught when you step into the paddock, rather than turning away from you. She may even go one step further and walk towards you.

Do Your Homework

Before you ever get to the point where the horse is in a larger space and you want to catch her, you should spend some time working on this in a smaller space such as a school arena or round pen. If the horse eludes you, make him work for his avoidance. Keep him moving around the pen, and every once in a while take a step back and see what you get. If the horse stops, great. If he stops and turns his head towards you, even better.

Your ultimate goal is for him to stop and turn his whole body towards you. This is the sign that he is ready to be caught, and you had better be ready to take this opening and catch him. If you don't, your horse will think maybe this isn't what you want, and you will lose your opportunity, making the next attempt even harder.

When you offer a step back for the horse to stop, there are a couple of other things that might happen as well. Here is a series of 'ifs':

· If the horse stops when you take the pressure off, step back another step or two and see whether you can get him to turn his head.
· If you get that, take another step or two back from his head and move in towards his flank, to see whether that will draw on his head enough while putting pressure on his rear to get him to move his body around away from you and face you.
· If you get this, you are doing very well.
· If at any of these stages he walks off, that's fine. In fact, encourage him to take a trip or two around the pen, and when you think he's thinking about how he'd perhaps like to not be doing this (maybe he holds an ear in your direction), give him another opportunity to step in. You will probably get his whole body this time.

This whole process can take 10 minutes or 90 minutes, and is worth working on a few times when you don't *need* to catch your horse.

A 'flag' makes a good extender for your arm and can add to your
presence when working with your horse. Use a length of stiff wire a
couple of metres long with a piece of bandanna-sized cloth attached to
the end. Make sure that the end of the wire is bent over so it can't poke
your horse, the handle is comfortable and easy to grip, and the flag is not
so heavy that your arm will tire.

Reminder

Always bear in mind that a horse can kick out a lot further than you
think. It is a good idea to let the horse know you are coming up behind
him. Talk to him or, if you are going from the front of the horse to the
back, keep your hand on the horse all the way around so that he can know
where you are. The traditional logic has been that if you stay close to the
horse's hind end, a kick won't have the full impact; or if you are back
almost far enough, you'll only get the tail end of the kick. DO NOT put
yourself in the line of fire. A flag is useful as an extension of your arm so
that you won't get within kicking distance; but in a confined situation,
such as a stable, it may frighten the horse too much. Get help until you
have enough experience to confidently handle these kinds of situations
(and by then, you'll find them coming up less and less).

Picking up the Feet

Teaching a horse to have her feet handled is something that needs to start
taking place early in the horse's life. This can be done gradually, and starts
with good handling in general. People think they are having trouble
picking up their horse's feet, when the trouble is in other parts of the
horse's handling and in his attitude towards humans; if these problems
are addressed, the horse's feet handling problems clear up, too.

To teach a young horse about having her feet handled, forget about
the feet for a while. Instead, while grooming the horse, start grooming the
legs and getting the horse used to having her legs touched and worked
with. Using grooming to get the horse accustomed to having his feet
worked with is common sense. This is a good start.

The Front Feet

Getting a horse's foot off the ground can be quite tricky (it's that self-preservation, always-be-prepared-for-flight thing). Often the front feet are easier to pick up than the back, perhaps because the horse can keep a better eye on you when you're in front of her. The human may also be more at ease with the front legs because they aren't the ones you get kicked with. Getting stepped on or pawed at or shoved out of the way is not a pleasant experience either, however. So be aware of what the horse is capable of doing when she feels she is being pushed to her limits.

Stand beside the horse's leg, facing the rear of the horse. Run your hand down the leg, and when you get towards the hoof, gently pull or squeeze or do something simple that might cause the horse to lift her foot. Hold the foot up for *just a couple of seconds* and put the foot back down. The key here is to put the foot back down before the horse snatches it back. Set the horse up to succeed – don't hold the foot so long that she simply can't stand it any longer. That just isn't fair.

Many experienced trainers spend part of their time touring the country, holding clinics and giving demonstrations of how they ride or handle horses. It is well worth attending these to see how other people work with horses. If you can't take your horse along, you can usually simply go and watch. Most of these events are advertised in horse magazines, the local press and tack shops.

If she doesn't let you pick the foot up in the first couple of tries, work at it in small increments and build on those – be satisfied the first few times with her shifting her weight, the next with her flexing, even if she doesn't actually lift her foot. Eventually, you will get the foot up.

And when I say put the foot back down, that is exactly what I mean – put it down. Don't just let go unexpectedly and let the horse's foot bang to the ground. If you do that, you'll find the horse reluctant to let you pick her foot up again. And if she does, she will snatch it away in anticipation of her foot banging to the ground. Give your horse this bit of respect, and make sure your farrier does, too!

The Back Feet

The back feet are similar to, but different from the front feet. Again, stand beside the leg facing the rear, and run your hand down the horse's leg to the hoof. Squeeze or gently pull to get the horse to lift her leg. When you first start to pick up back legs, just get the hoof off the ground, hold it for a second and place it back down.

Eventually, you will work towards holding the back leg up and out, using your thigh to help support it. However, you should also be teaching your horse to hold up its own weight while one foot is raised; your farrier will expect this as well.

Your Horse and the Farrier

It is your job to get your horse accustomed to having her feet handled, not your farrier's. Don't forget to gradually get her to lift one foot off the ground for longer and longer periods of time. With this kind of exposure, your farrier should have little problem in trimming your horse's feet.

Add to your foot work a simple simulation of shoeing by gently tapping on the outer edge of the horse's hoof with something like a hoof pick. Although this is helpful, nothing quite matches the experience of having shoes nailed on her feet! Your farrier might be able to show you some positions to practise, to help your horse become accustomed to this handling before the farrier adds the complication of shoeing.

Some horses never have a problem with shoeing. More frequently, horses simply need a few shoeings to become accustomed to this experience. With astute handling from both you and your farrier, your horse will soon learn to stand quietly.

Loading in a Trailer or Horsebox

Ah, the horse trailer, often the bane of the horse owner's existence. With a little work on your part, loading your horse can be a stroll in the park. After attending numerous horse clinics where good handling was taught, and where trailer-loading demonstrations were always amazing, I have come to enjoy teaching horses to be loaded onto trailers.

Choosing a Trailer or Horsebox

Unless you have several horses that you are forever taking all over the place, a trailer is probably your best option. Horseboxes have the advantage that they are all in one piece, which can make manoeuvring them easier, but they can spend a lot of time sitting around unused at home, and this is expensive, considering they must still have road tax and pass their MOT test and so on. A trailer is easy to hitch up when you need it, and is not liable for road tax or MOT testing, although you must check it for roadworthiness each time you use it.

Whatever you choose, make sure it is an appropriate size for your horse or horses. You are asking a lot of a flighty animal to go into a small enclosed space and then to be swung around corners and sped along roads for minutes or hours at a time, so think about your horse's comfort. A light, airy trailer with a front ramp as well as a back one is ideal. Make sure that it is fairly stable, so it doesn't rock around too much when you are loading and moving the horse. Ramps with a gentle incline are preferable to steep slopes, and with a reluctant loader it can be useful to have gates at the back that, when open, enclose the sides of the ramp, making the horse less likely to jump off them.

Some horses prefer to travel loose in a trailer or box and will actually turn around and face backwards if given the choice. If you think your horse might be happier this way, have your trailer checked to ensure that it is safe to do this, as the weight distribution will be different.

Make sure that your vehicle is capable of towing the trailer. It is dangerous to overload your engine and will render your insurance invalid, too. If you are not sure about its towing power, get in contact with the manufacturers, and they will be able to advise you. Finally, if you passed your driving test after 1 January 1997, you need to take an additional test to be able to tow anything over 3,500kg (7,700lb), including the weight of your tow vehicle.

The Ultimate Test: Load Her Up!

Loading a horse onto a trailer is the ultimate test of how well you've refined all the groundwork you've done with your horse thus far. If you have done a thorough job, loading should go pretty smoothly. If your horse is the easygoing, forgiving type, your groundwork may not even have to be all that thorough. If the horse is overanxious and not as easily trusting of your intentions, you will have to spend a little more time refining your groundwork before you get to loading.

When loading young horses or any horse for the first time, it's wise to have someone around in case you get into trouble. You want someone there in case of a problem, but not actually helping – this is your party. Make sure that the person is patient and respects your approach to handling your animals.

Make sure the trailer you use is exceedingly safe – that there are no sharp protrusions to get cut on or odd places for a lead rope to get caught.

Before loading her up, put a halter on your horse. Make sure that it has a fairly long lead rope – 3.6m (12ft) is OK, but 4.8m (16ft) would be better. I suggest putting a haynet in the trailer, not as a bribe to get her in but as a comforting thing to greet her when she does. If the hay offers one more incentive for her to get in, great, but you should in fact be careful not to entice her onto the trailer physically before she's mentally ready to be there.

Lead your horse to the trailer and let her check things out. Keep the gate open and let her look and smell inside. As long as her attention is on the trailer, let her do this investigating. If you sense that she is becoming interested in things outside the trailer, do what it takes to return her attention back inside – send some energy up the lead rope, or actually lead her back to the entrance if you have to.

Basically, as long as her attention is on that trailer, everything will be quiet and calm. If her attention leaves the trailer, things will get busy. If you have done your groundwork well up to this point and your timing and consistency are good, she will soon realize that the trailer is a good place to be, as that's where things are calm and peaceful.

If you are new to the concept of groundwork and need some ideas for things to do, *Groundwork: Training for Your Horse* by Lesley Bailey (published by David & Charles) is full of a variety of ideas and approaches, and covers conventional techniques in groundwork, as well as the methods used by 'natural' horsemen.

Don't Rush!

Once she is calmly looking inside, ask her to take a step up by gently tapping her on the rump with the end of the lead rope. *Don't rush this stage.* The last thing you want to do is have the horse thinking of the trailer as a peaceful place, and then ruin that idea. You should neither expect nor want her to go all the way in at this point. If she puts her two front feet in, let her live with that idea for a second, then ask her to back out before she decides to back out herself. Do this a few times until you feel this has gone in. If there is no other option but to back out, you will want to do this step several times until you are confident that she knows the way out is by backing up.

The next step will be getting all four feet onto the trailer. If she puts all four in but backs right out, that's OK. If she rushes out and is a little excited, calm her down, rub her, talk to her first, then ask her to step onto it again. Don't expect her to walk right onto the trailer and settle in and eat that hay. She may grab a bite and come flying back out, or she may feel uncomfortable going that far. This is all just practice, so you are in absolutely no hurry. In fact, you may want to just get to stage one for a few sessions and move onto the next stage some other day.

The first few times she puts all four feet onto the trailer, you can get up into the trailer with her and help her feel more comfortable. At some point, she is going to go in every time you ask her and walk up to the hay. *Again, don't rush.* Let her learn to relax in there. This is where people often start to rush ('OK, she's in, slam the door shut!') and then ruin all their good work, betray the horse and in many instances create a good wreck in the process. I've heard sad tales of horses who were rushed into trailers before they were ready and came flying back with enough force to knock themselves over backwards, hit their head and die – as fast as that. Don't be in a hurry; it just isn't worth it – it will end up taking longer.

Shutting Her In

Wait until your horse has proven that she's calm and relaxed standing in the trailer, munching some hay. If she starts to back up, you can tap her on the rump with the lead rope or your hand to get her to step back up to the front – no big deal. If she eats hay and props up one back leg to relax, all the better. Gently but efficiently lift the ramp and then close it. If she raises her head and checks out what's going on behind her but doesn't freak out about it, you've done a good job. A horse who learns about the trailer in this way will make your horse life much easier. Tie her at the head, and be sure to untie her first before lowering the ramp.

Towing a Trailer

First, make sure your vehicle is powerful enough (see page 178). Check the owner's manual to see how it is rated for towing; don't just slap a tow bar on it and go. The vehicle needs an engine strong enough to be able to pull the trailer and its contents up any hill you may come across, and should have a transmission cooling system to help the engine alleviate excess heat from the strain of towing.

When towing a horse trailer, the key is to always drive slower than you think you need to. The horse can easily be tossed around if you have to make any sudden moves.

Good Handling, Good Horse

Good handling results in horses who are a joy to be around. Things such as loading, foot work and worming go a lot smoother. And if they don't go smoothly, you at least have some tools to fall back on to improve the situation.

Don't rely on gimmicks and quick fixes; take the time to learn good horsemanship and good handling. That knowledge will be with you for the rest of your life.

CHAPTER 12

Types of Horsemanship

A common question asked by people when they find out you have a horse is, 'What do you do with your horse?' You may not have an interest in 'doing' anything. Riding or caring for your horse gets you outdoors and provides you with some exercise, and that, with the social environment of other riders, is really what you enjoy in your horse life.

But for thousands of horse owners this is not enough. They either got into horses to be involved in a specific equine activity, or they became interested in a specific activity shortly after they became involved with horses. And it's not uncommon to go through more than one type of horsemanship interest during your horse career.

Lots of Possibilities

You may already have an idea of what kind of riding and horsemanship appeal to you. Maybe you have a friend who goes to horse shows every weekend and seems to have a lot of fun. Perhaps you have gone on a few hacks on holiday in the summer, and nothing seems more relaxing to you than strolling along bridleways on the back of a horse. Or you might be the kind of person who likes a faster pace, and so fox hunting or polo seem to be right for you. Whatever your interest or inclination, there is a horse activity and type of horsemanship to match it, including ones that don't involve riding at all!

The website for the British Horse Society is *www.bhs.org.uk*. You'll find information about becoming a member, local riding groups and activities and much more, as well as other horsey information.

Jumping

There are two basic ways to become involved in jumping:

1. **Showjumping:** this is where the jumps are set up within the confines of a show arena. This can be a class in a show, a show in itself or one of the three legs of a one- or three-day event. Riders are expected to follow a specific predetermined pattern around the jump course. Your run around the course is timed, and faults are given for any rails knocked over.

   Showjumping classes are held at all local and county shows, along with all the showing classes and the various other competitions. Even if you don't fancy the serious classes at smaller shows, there is usually a clear round jumping course, where the jumps are raised and lowered during the day and you simply see whether you can get around without knocking any jumps down. Riding clubs and other equestrian organizations also hold jumping competitions of varying difficulty.

2. **Cross-country:** as with jumping, cross-country jumping can be an event in itself or one of the parts of a one- or three-day event. The jump course is set up in a 'cross-country' setting through woods and fields. There is a specific course to follow, judges are stationed at each jump, and your run is timed. Depending on where you live, you may have access to a cross-country course that you can pay to use for practice or just for fun, or someone in your area may arrange regular cross-country events.

Dressage

The French word *dressage* basically means 'training'. In dressage competition, someone is basically showing off the level of training of his or her horse. The training is not for battle or to drive a carriage. In fact, it has become an end in itself, and riders now 'do dressage' as an equestrian activity. It is taken quite seriously, requiring years and years of discipline and practice.

Dressage competitions are different from the typical 'horse show'. For one thing, although you are still competing against a group of other riders, you compete in the ring alone. On the one hand, you don't need to worry about other riders around you and can concentrate on your own performance; on the other hand, you are alone out there, and all eyes are on you. Once you gain experience and become comfortable with dressage itself, you will become so focused on your performance that you won't even think about the 'all eyes are on you' aspect of your test.

Get to the show well in advance to get your horse ready, settled and warmed up. Sometimes the tests before yours move along faster than their allotted time, and you may be able to do your test earlier than planned; but you can still stick to your given time if you want to.

What are rails?
Rails are the individual horizontal bars that make up a jump. They can be easily removed or added to make the jump lower or higher.

Beginning dressage riders and their mounts start at preliminary level and progress through the next five levels of dressage: novice, elementary, medium, advanced medium, and advanced, which includes the Prix St Georges. Once you have graduated beyond one level and have begun working in the next, you and your trainer may decide that your horse is not the right horse in mind and/or body to take you to the next level of competition. It may be like expecting your trusty hatchback to take you from its current job, driving to and from work, which it does quite well, to entering the Monte Carlo Rally. This is where horsemanship gets a long way beyond pleasure riding, and you will need to make some decisions regarding your goals as an equestrian.

Do you want to spend years and years on this horse, or is it time to get something more suitable? Is it this horse that is the most important to you, or is it dressage competition? Maybe you would love to see your nicely trained elementary-level horse in the hands of a young competitor. Or maybe it's time to take the same horse and do something different. I'm not suggesting one choice is better or worse than another, but it is probably what you will come up against if you progress through the stages of dressage competition (and to get to any competition's highest levels).

Eventing

Events are held on one day or over three days. In both cases, a horse and rider team have to do a dressage test, then complete a rigorous cross-country course and finally do a showjumping round. In three-day events, roads and tracks and steeplechasing are thrown in for good measure on the cross-country day, so by the showjumping day you and your horse might have covered some 20 miles at fast speeds. If you are keen on eventing, it is vital that you and your horse are extremely fit, although at the lower levels of one-day events the endurance factor is not so important.

Fox hunting

Although its future is uncertain, there are still plenty of people who enjoy fox hunting for the speed and excitement of the baying hounds and the galloping horses. It also offers the chance to see countryside that you might not otherwise be able to ride over. It is also a good way to expose your horse to lots of other horses in an exciting atmosphere.

Endurance

Endurance rides are a test of a horse and rider's stamina and fitness. It takes a lot of preplanning, conditioning and preparation to complete an endurance course of 80 or 160km (50 or 100 miles), such as the Golden Horseshoe, which takes place on Exmoor each year. Most people think of endurance horses being Arabs or Arab crosses, but in fact, in the lower levels of the competition, any fit horse will be quite capable of finishing a course, and many do very well.

If you think you might like to try endurance, it would be a good idea to go on some pleasure rides, which are held all over the country throughout the spring and summer. They are usually up to about 25 miles or less and require only a reasonably fit horse. You can usually do them at your own pace, which means that you can see how your horse does without having to push her too hard. When you get into the more serious competitions, you will need to have a whole team of people helping you to get through the rigours of the course.

The Golden Horseshoe, which is Britain's best-known endurance competition, was moved to Exmoor in 1974, having previously been held all over the country. The course covers 160km (100 miles) over two days in May, and is very gruelling. To enter the full Golden Horseshoe you have to do qualifying rides of about 65km (40 miles), but other, shorter, competitions are usually also held at the same time. See *www.goldenhorseshoe.co.uk* for more details.

Games

Polo

Polo's real heyday was in the 1930s, but the last 20 years have seen a resurgence in popularity. Polo is a fast-paced game played on a field 160m (525ft) wide and 300m (985ft) long; it is played in six seven-minute 'chukkers' or 'chukkas' over approximately 90 minutes. To compete, you need to have access to numerous polo ponies. (Polo ponies are not a breed; they are compact, usually short, horses who have been exposed to the idea of having mallet-wielding riders on their backs.) You must be a confident and extremely balanced rider in order to make quick turns and gallop for most of the game.

To find a club near you, learn all the rules of the game, and obtain lots more information about polo, check the UK Polo website at *www.uk-polo.co.uk*.

Polocrosse

Polocrosse is a sister sport to polo that originated in Persia hundreds of years ago. The game is organized quite like polo, but with some key differences: for example, each rider uses only one horse and sits out chukkers to catch his or her breath, and the ball is moved with a racket, not a mallet.

there are many polocrosse clubs all around Britain; for a club near you, contact the UK Polocrosse Association on *www.polocrosse.org.uk*.

Gymkhanas

Gymkhanas are closely associated with the Pony Club (*www.pony-club.org.uk*); a more modern term for them is mounted games. The Pony Club has about 40,000 members in Britain alone and is an extremely good place for a youngster, up to the age of 21, to get involved with all sorts of equestrian activities.

Gymkhanas are competitive games on horseback. They are usually won or lost solely on timing. In barrel racing, for instance, a horse and rider go as fast as possible around a group of barrels at the end of an arena. The team must follow a very specific pattern regarding which side to approach the barrel on and what barrel to go to next. This is a strictly timed event, with time points taken off and elimination for knocking over barrels, going off course or using unsanctioned equipment. A similar activity is pole bending, in which the horse and rider need to weave around tall poles following a specific pattern.

Mounted games are just one aspect of the Pony Club, which also aims to give members a good grounding in all aspects of riding and keeping horses. If you like gymkhanas and mounted games you will already know that the exciting final to the year's competitions is the Prince Philip Cup, held annually at the Horse of the Year Show.

Showing

Horse showing is probably the most common horse activity. It has something for everyone – beginner and advanced rider alike, in hand or under saddle.

You must understand up front that the horse show world is competitive and can be expensive, even at local levels. If you think you are interested, you should be sure you are fully prepared to make the commitment of time and money that is required to be successful, which means, of course, winning ribbons or placing.

You may be thinking, 'Oh, I don't care about winning ribbons. I just like to go to the shows.' Don't kid yourself. Horse shows are about competing, and competing successfully means placing above as many of the other horse and human teams as possible. Good or bad, it's as simple as that. Don't get me wrong; that doesn't mean that it doesn't entail good sportsmanship. It certainly should! And it is true that competing in horse shows, whether you win ribbons or not, can be personally rewarding, depending on the goals you set for yourself. Maybe you consider a show successful if your horse gets through one class without going out of control. Maybe the next show is successful if your horse gets through the entire day calmly and without upset. But at some point, the show competitor expects his or her team to win a ribbon. And to do that, the team needs to be competitive in the circuit in which they are showing.

In order to be relaxed and ready to show, it's important to arrive fully prepared. Here are some things you won't want to be without:

For the horse:

- First aid kit
- Saddle(s) and pad(s)
- Leg wraps
- Bridle(s)
- Grooming equipment and products

- Hay and feed
- Feed and water buckets
- Rug(s)
- Fly spray

For the rider:

- Clean clothes for almost every class you signed up for
- Helmet
- Hairpins and hairnets
- Riding boots

- Comfortable shoes for before and after the show
- Rain gear
- Personal items

Average-sized local horse shows are made up of several classes that might last for 15–20 minutes and have up to 25 riders. The classes may be purely show classes, where you and your horse are judged on your appearance, conformation and general turnout, or they may involve going through the paces and perhaps doing a short display on your own. If you are new to showing, the best thing to do is talk to the show organizers to find out which classes you would most like to do, or go along to one or two on foot and watch what the other competitors do. At some shows, the competition is very fierce; at others, the riders are going along just as much for a fun day out as to win rosettes. Classes are arranged according to experience, so there is something for everyone.

1. **Tack and turnout classes:** these are based mostly on the appearance of the horse and rider and how smart they both are.
2. **Riding classes:** these classes are judged both on conformation and ridden manners.
3. **Working hunter classes:** these involve going through the paces and doing a small jump.
4. **Other classes:** some classes are restricted to a particular type of horse – **best ridden cob**, for example. Many smaller shows also have more informal classes, such as **best family pony** and **best veteran**.
5. **Gymkhana events:** all local shows will have gymkhana events, such as bending races and musical poles.

How to be Competitive – the Horse

You don't need a specific kind of horse to become part of the show world unless you are interested in breed-specific shows; almost all the breeds have their own breed shows. If you are buying a horse with the intention of showing it, you should pay particular attention to conformation. Conformation flaws won't eliminate you, but it is an advantage to have a mount that is put together well.

Training

How does your horse need to be trained to compete? Whether you agree with the style or not, your horse needs to move the way everyone else is moving, which means it will have to be on the bit to get anywhere – and the current fashion is for horses to be rather overbent.

The chances are that you want to win some competitions, so teaching your horse the correct style for the class you are in is crucial. You need to spend some time schooling your horse to teach it what it needs to know; however, you also need to know how to teach your horse in the first place – Chapters 11 and 14 cover this in more depth. But ultimately, training a horse to compete in horse shows is a long process that cannot be learned from a book.

In the show world, there is an appropriate etiquette – how and when to pass a horse who is slower, for example – and your instructor/trainer can help you learn these things. The rules can be different for each kind of show and type of riding. Make sure you know which rules apply to the show you're entering.

Beyond Your Yard

If you plan to participate in shows more competitive than your local riding club fun shows – either regional or national – then you will probably need to work with a trainer to succeed. The trainer for your discipline will know all the rules, all the current accepted styles and where all the shows are – and many are well known to the judges. Many riders who get serious about horse showing keep their show horse at a trainer's yard, pay the trainer to continue to work with their horse, take regular lessons from the trainer and travel with the trainer and the trainer's other students to the shows, or they do all this with a horse that is owned by their trainer. Whatever you decide, make sure that your bank account for your horse activities is well in the black. It may be well within your price range, but you need to know that there will be constant costs.

There are also many administrative things to keep track of, such as registering for the show, picking classes, paying for classes, asking for tack change breaks between classes if they are allowed and bringing vaccine records as needed for your horse.

How to be Competitive – the Rider

In order to be competitive in the show ring, you need to constantly upgrade and refine your riding skills, on your own and with an instructor.

If you get into horse shows for a long time, you may also need to occasionally consider changing horses as your competitive needs change. Some horses are not suited for the pressures of showing – which include long hours in the trailer travelling to an event, a constant changing of environment, long periods of time confined to a stall or tied to the side of the trailer, and going around and around a show ring. This can cause a lot of stress for some horses; even those who used to like showing can 'burn out' and need a break or permanent retirement from the show ring.

Attend one or two regional shows as a spectator before you decide to compete in one. That way, you can get a feel for the atmosphere and whether you can ever be comfortable competing at that level.

Local Shows

Local riding clubs are lots of fun and are a great way to accumulate some horse friends for people who keep their horses at home and don't get the advantage of the built-in peer group that you get when you keep your horse at a livery yard. Local shows are also good places for beginners to get over some early show jitters (both rider and horse!) before venturing into the more competitive arenas. The shows are smaller, which means that there are fewer horses and smaller classes and, therefore, that you might be able to build your confidence and win some ribbons early on. Fewer people can mean as much cameraderie as competitiveness. Local shows and clubs also offer the opportunity to widen your circle of horse friends by volunteering to help in any number of capacities, from club treasurer to ring steward, or simply to tidy up the ring and grounds after a show.

Regional Shows

Regional shows are often held as part of a county agricultural show, or they may be devoted entirely to horses. They are quite large, and the competition is much tougher – in numbers and in skill level. These types of shows might be a good next step after spending some time showing locally.

National Shows

The shows put on nationally are highly competitive and mostly well-attended. It is really not worth the time and money to attend one of these with your horse unless you have spent the energy in thorough preparation, probably gaining experience in local and regional shows first. It's a good opportunity to talk to some other competitors about their experiences showing at the national shows. And if it all sounds exciting, then by all means go for it! (For a discussion of the different riding classes you will find at horse shows, see Chapter 14.)

In-Hand Classes

In-hand horses typically compete against each other by age group and are judged on conformation. For example, are her legs and feet of a sufficient size compared to her body? Is her neck nicely built without an overall structural flaw, such as getting very narrow towards the head? In breed-specific shows, horses are competing against their own breed; in larger non-breed shows, there will often be different classes for different horses of the predominating breeds.

For showing in-hand, your horse must be impeccably groomed, and you should follow the style of the moment. Are horses' hooves being painted black, or is *au naturel* in this year? How are manes being groomed? For mountain and moorland breeds as well as Arabs, the manes are usually left long and natural, while for other breeds and classes plaiting is the norm. Whatever you do, make sure you accentuate your horse's good points and play down her bad ones. Judges won't be fooled, but the overall picture will look better.

The other thing about horses being shown in-hand is that in the big shows, horses are selectively bred for looks not riding, so the traits that are 'in' for a few years when it comes to in-hand classes may not be the best traits for riding the horse. While this is important to think about, showing in-hand can be fun for someone who wants to be involved in horses but doesn't want to ride.

Natural Horsemanship

In the past 15–20 years, an approach to teaching and riding horses has been, for better or worse, tagged Natural Horsemanship. It came to Britain from the United States, where a few horsemen had started going around holding hands-on educational clinics that showed people how to start young horses under saddle using a more sensitive approach to the methods that predominated for the better part of the 19th and 20th centuries. These trainers, who included the well-known Monty Roberts, also showed people how to communicate more meaningfully with their older horses who were already under saddle. Teaching the human about how to *educate* their horse through feel, rather than *train* them in a mechanical way, has become a popular activity.

With the novel *The Horse Whisperer* by Nicholas Evans, and the subsequent film directed by and starring Robert Redford, and an increasing number of practitioners, this approach has become much more widespread. However, the original intention – which is really not new – has sometimes got a bit lost along the way.

The basic premise of this different way of working with horses is this: instead of forcing their natural instincts out of them and creating a horse that is submissive to humans, horses are treated as the thinking, living beings that they are – they are educated, not trained, and that education is accomplished through working with those natural instincts (such as herd dynamics).

Kelly Marks, Richard Maxwell, Michael Peace and Ross Simpson are well-known British proponents of 'natural' horsemanship. However, they all have slightly different approaches to horses, so you need to look into their methods to decide which you prefer. They all regularly contribute to horse magazines and have written books on the subject, as well as holding demonstrations around the country. Here are a couple of website addresses: Michael Peace *www.thinkequus.com*; Ross Simpson *www.naturalanimalcentre.com*.

If you are willing to spend a lot of time working at this approach, it can result in a horse that works in a relaxed frame of mind and has learned to be respectful of its handler. When learning new things, the horse can be comfortable searching for the answer without being worried that a wrong answer is going to result in some painful punishment. And horses who respect their rider/handler and come to look to him or her for support are more apt to put some of their natural reactions aside and instead trust their handler/rider to help them through new situations.

One of the keys to success in dealing with your horse this way is to perfect your timing and be consistent in your interactions with the horse, especially in his early education. If you give the horse one message at one time and a different one the next, he will become confused and frustrated. If you are totally inconsistent, the horse whose personality is very forgiving will fill in for your inadequacies and get along as best she can (many horses are exactly this way, which is the only reason so many people get along as well as they do with horses). But the horse who is not as forgiving of your lack of timing and consistency – well, let's just say that that horse will be the impetus that drives you to one of these trainers.

This is a simplistic explanation for something that takes a few lifetimes to learn. But if it intrigues you, as it has me, it will provide you with at least one lifetime of learning.

Western Riding

You don't have to go to the United States to enjoy Western riding; there are plenty of people who ride Western-style in Britain. Western riding is associated with cowboys and cattle, but it is also a very comfortable way to ride for long distances, as it is more relaxed than traditional classical riding, which is what we mostly do in Britain. Quarter horses are the breed of choice for serious Western riding, but if you simply want to ride in a more relaxed way, then any breed will do.

One of the major differences you will notice when Western riding is that you don't keep the horse on a close contact with the reins. The reins tend to be quite loose unless the rider wants to direct the horse in some way. As soon as the horse responds to the request, they are loosened again. Neck reining is another key difference. This is where the horse is manoeuvred by resting the reins on one side of the neck. It is amazing how quickly even a classically trained horse will pick up on this technique – try it with your horse and see. Legs and your weight are also important in Western riding, and as you become more proficient they will take over from using the reins in many cases. A Western horse can be asked to halt, turn and change pace with the legs and body weight.

There are various Western riding disciplines. Reining is perhaps the best-known and is almost like a version of dressage, in that the horse is expected to perform quite complicated movements willingly and athletically with very subtle signals from the rider. Reining is done at the lope (canter) and includes the spectacular sliding stop and the spin (a 360° turn on the hindquarters).

For more information, visit the following websites: *www.aqha.co.uk* (UK American Quarter Horse Association) and *www.britishreining.co.uk* (British Reining Horse Association).

Racing

Horse racing is perhaps the most popular equine event known to the average person. The chances that you will ride a racehorse as a jockey are slim. If you want to be involved, you need to be serious and dedicated, and start spending time at the racing stables now!

Racing isn't just for Thoroughbreds, although they still make up the majority of the races and certainly the most glamorous ones, including the Derby, Oaks and 3,000 Guineas. Arabs have a racing circuit, too.

Flat racing (think Epsom Derby) refers to the under-saddle kind of racing that most of us know. Racing on horseback – and the gambling that goes with it – has been around since ancient times, and it's not going away any time soon!

Steeplechasing – which combines flat racing and jumping – is best known by the Grand National event at Aintree, near Liverpool, which has taken place since 1839. The event started out with three jumps. Now it includes 30 fences and 40 horses, many of whom do not complete the race. The course is run twice for a total of 7.2km (4.5 miles), with 16 jumps on the first round and 14 on the second.

In harness racing, which is very popular in the USA, the horse pulls the human in a cart.

Don't Forget the Fun!

You certainly won't be able to fit each type of horsemanship into your riding career (and this isn't even an exhaustive list!), even if you were to spend a lifetime trying. Be sure of your chosen activity before you kit yourself and your horse out with every piece of equipment for that activity. And don't get so serious that you forget to have fun, especially if you originally got involved in horses for recreation.

CHAPTER 13

Tack and Accessories

As with any sport, activity, interest or hobby, you can easily collect a lot of 'stuff' when you are involved with horses. There are millions of items for you, the rider, as well as for your horse, to choose from. And if you keep your horse at home, there are a million more items you can collect to enhance your stable.

Stable supplies and equipment are covered in Chapter 6, and medical supplies for your horse are covered in Chapter 9. This chapter covers the items you need or may want to have, both to handle and ride your horse.

Equipment and Accessories for the Horse

Some of these items you just have to have; others simply come in handy. If you are a beginner, realize that in time you will develop your preferences for materials and types of equipment; sometimes it just takes trial and error, and no matter how frugal you are about collecting, you may end up with things you find you don't like or don't really need.

If you'd like to get rid of items you no longer need, look for tack shops that sell used equipment, find a pony club or equine charity that is looking for donations, or set up a tack table top or car boot sale.

Handling Equipment

Halters

First and foremost, you will need a halter and a lead rope. You will establish your preferences for what these are made of as you become more experienced. Basically, there are three kinds of halters:

- **Leather halters:** if you are going to buy a leather halter, buy one that is top quality. The fittings should be brass and the leather soft and strong. The seams should be properly double-stitched, not screwed or tacked together.
- **Web halters:** made of nylon webbing, these halters are the most common and least expensive. They come in a variety of colours. Web halters also come in breakaway models, which have one leather piece that will break in a major struggle.
- **Rope halters:** rope halters are made of marine or rock climbing-type ropes and are great for young horses being taught by effective handlers, or for pushy horses and less-than-effective handlers. The thinner rope has a bit more 'bite' than the web halters, which spread the pressure over a wider area.

Lead Ropes

Lead ropes are usually around 3.6–4.8m (8–12ft) long for general use, and are usually made of cotton, flat webbing or polypropylene. You can also get leather ones for showing, although these are not really suitable for everyday use. The important thing is how the lead rope feels in your hand.

Stay away from lead ropes with lengths of chain on the end; they are intended to wrap around the horse's nose for better control. However, if you teach your horses to be respectful at the end of the lead, you will not need the chain, which just gets in the way in regular use.

Lunging Equipment

If you plan to exercise your horse on the ground by lunging before riding or instead of riding, you will need approximately 10m (33ft) of line and probably a lunge whip. Lunge lines are readily available for £5–10, and it's worth getting a line designed for horse handling. If the lunge rein has a loop on the end, be sure not to put your hand right through it, and never loop the rein around you hand. This is extremely dangerous should the horse decide to bolt while it is on the lunge.

Lunge whips are standard tall whips with a long snapper. They are inexpensive, and often help you make just the right triangle (horse, line from his head to you, whip from you to his rear) to keep your horse moving forward on the circle. Lunge whips are not intended to be used to actually hit the horse.

Long Reins

Many people who train young horses often use long reins to teach the horse about the bit and reins before the horse is even started under saddle. Driving reins are attached to a bridle and run through the stirrups, which are secured under the horse, allowing the person to walk behind the horse, driving the horse from the rear as if driving a cart.

Riding Equipment

Saddles

If you are going to ride your horse, you will need a saddle – probably the most important and most expensive piece of equipment that you will buy for your horse. It is vital that the saddle fits properly and comfortably and distributes your weight evenly across the horse's back. A saddle can make the difference between a fit, healthy and happy horse and one that goes badly when ridden and hates to be tacked up.

Although good-quality saddles are expensive, you will never regret spending money on one that fits properly. Arrange to have a fully qualified saddler fit a saddle on your horse, and make sure that he or she knows exactly what you intend to do with her. Synthetic saddles can be extremely comfortable and are comparatively cheap, but leather ones last longer and are more likely to mould to the horse's shape, and your own.

Saddles basically come in three types: dressage, jumping or general-purpose.

1. **Dressage:** the design of this saddle is intended to keep the rider's legs fairly straight underneath them for the more upright position of dressage riding.
2. **Jumping:** as the name implies, this is the type of saddle you would choose if you were interested in jumping activities (cross-country riding or showjumping). The saddles are designed for a more forward seat and a more bent leg, and they have varying degrees of knee rolls for the bent knee to rest on.

A shopping trip to a used tack shop can provide the beginner with almost everything she needs to get started. Most horse equipment is made to wear extremely well, so many used items are in extremely good condition. A reputable shop will clean everything up and be honest about any required repairs. The classified ads can require more running around, but you can often find bargains if you know what you are looking for.

FIGURE 13.1:
Saddle

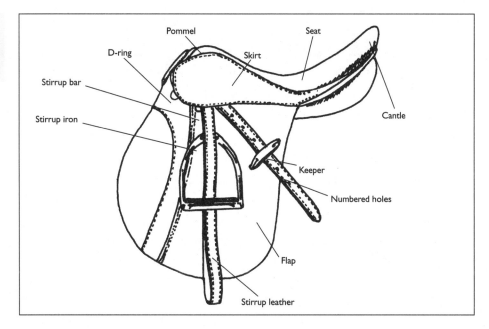

3. **General-purpose:** intended for the general rider, these saddles are suitable for novice jumping and dressage, as well as for hacking.

If you already have a saddle, check whether it fits. Here are some things to look out for:

- After a ride, look at the bottom of the saddle pad. Is it unevenly dirty? Are there odd hair patterns, swirling or flattened areas that indicate uneven and misplaced pressure?
- When you groom your horse, does she drop her back away from your hand?
- Are there any sore spots, white hairs, or bumps where the saddle comes in contact with her?
- Does she show agitated behaviour when you are about to saddle her?
- Does she move in a constrained way under saddle but fluidly loose?

These aren't necessarily indications of poor saddle fit, but they certainly could be.

If you want to learn more about saddle fitting, the book *Saddle Fitting* by Kay Humphries (Allen Photographic Guide 15) is very thorough. Two useful websites are *www.saddle-fitting.com* and *www.free-and-easy-saddles.co.uk/saddle-fitting.htm*.

Saddle Construction

All saddles are made around a basic structure called a tree, which can be made of wood or fibreglass and other synthetic (and often lighter-weight) materials. The tree can be wider or narrower, depending on the size of the horse – cobs tend to be wide, whereas many Thoroughbreds are fairly narrow. The rider's major concern when it comes to the saddle tree is the twist, which is the degree of slant in the sloped area in the front of the saddle tree. The steeper the slant, the narrower the saddle will feel to the rider. The length of the saddle is also important, with larger riders requiring longer saddles.

Girths

Girths are made of leather or webbing or a combination of materials. Leather girths come in a variety of styles, including Atherstone and Balding, both of which are shaped to fit behind the forelegs. Girths made of other materials tend to be unshaped. All girths have buckles at both ends, and these fasten onto billet straps on the saddle, keeping the saddle in place. Some girths have a section of elastic on one side; this makes them easier to do up and means they have a little bit of give, which is more comfortable for the horse. Leather girths last longer and look smarter, but webbing ones are often more supple and can be put in the washing machine to be cleaned.

A Western girth is called a cinch, and can be made of many materials, including leather, neoprene or webbing, or a combination. Look for a cinch with small rings on either side of the middle for attaching accessories such as breast collars and belly straps (for rear cinches).

Breast Plates

A breast plate is used to hold the saddle in place and prevent it from slipping back, especially during jumping. Breast plates are usually made from leather. They consist of three connected pieces. Two of these attach to the D-rings on either side of the front of the saddle, and then the third runs between the horse's front legs where its loop is slipped over the girth.

A breast collar is a simplified version of a breast plate and loops under the horse's neck from one D-ring to the other. It is very useful when saddling a young horse for the first time, just to make sure that if it bucks the saddle doesn't slip backwards and scare it.

What is a tree?
A **tree** is the basic structure, usually made of wood or fibreglass, upon which both English and Western saddles are built. Trees can be narrow or wide, depending on the type of horse and the comfort of the rider.

Numnahs

A numnah is placed between the saddle and the horse's back to protect the horse from being chafed. As with everything else, there are many types of numnahs to choose from. Most follow the shape of the saddle, with very little pad exposed, and are often made of polycotton, cotton or fleece. Square-quilted cotton saddle cloths used more with dressage saddles come in many colours and fabrics, and can be customized with monograms and yard logos in the corners. They have nylon billets and girth straps to fit them to the saddle and keep them in place.

Contemporary materials have brought about the gel-cushion numnah and temperature-sensitive foam, which are designed to be therapeutic in nature. Pads, inserts and risers can be used to adjust saddles that don't fit the horse quite well enough, but, of course, it is always better to have the saddle fit well without them.

Keeping numnahs clean is a necessity for the comfort and health of your horse. Most can be put in the washing machine and allowed to dry fairly quickly.

Bridles and Other Tack

The entire headstall – bit, throat lash, cheek pieces and reins – is known as the bridle. The bridle's main function is to keep the bit in the horse's mouth.

FIGURE 13.3:
Bridle

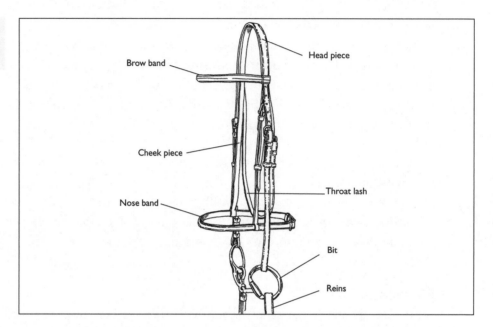

Brow band

Head piece

Cheek piece

Nose band

Throat lash

Bit

Reins

Choosing the right bit is very important. Although it would take a separate book to go into the different bits that are out there, I feel compelled to say up front that a lot of the bits you will see in tack shops and tack catalogues are not suitable for beginners. Your money is better spent learning better horsemanship than buying bits to increase the pressure you put on your horse's mouth.

A snaffle is basically a jointed piece of metal that goes in the horse's mouth and is attached to the reins with either O-shaped rings that can slide loosely around the ends of the bit, or D-shaped rings that stay stationary. Snaffle bits are the best educational bit for the horse at any age and for the everyday rider. They are the mildest bit (although any bit can be harsh when in harsh hands) and allow the horse to think about what you are trying to teach her, rather than the pain she is experiencing in her mouth.

The bit is a communication tool between you and your horse. When you pick up the reins and the bit comes in contact with the corners of the horse's mouth, the horse should be taught to understand that this means something. Although what it means can vary with the type of riding and horsemanship you learn and the level of education of your horse, the most common thing pressure from the bit means to a horse is to slow down or stop. You will eventually learn to communicate this to your horse in other ways – for example, by getting heavier in your seat and having less energy in your body – but the bit will always be one more communication tool.

The only bit you will probably ever need is a snaffle bit. If your horse is giving you problems and someone recommends that you get a harsher bit, find someone else to get your riding advice from.

Western-style bits with long shanks might look the authentic part if you are into Western riding, but a snaffle is still the most appropriate bit for general use.

The other parts of the bridle consist of the cheek pieces and headpiece, which hold the bit at the right height in the horse's mouth. The browband stops the bridle slipping backwards along the horse's poll and neck, and the throat lash prevents it from slipping forwards and off the horse's head. The nose band comes in a variety of styles. The basic cavesson is more or less decorative only, although it does stop the horse opening her mouth too wide; other nose bands stop horses evading the bit and crossing their jaws, but most of these riding problems can be solved through good schooling.

Martingales are a common sight on many horses. They are used to prevent a horse getting its head too high in the air, which will allow it to evade requests you send via the bit. There are two types: running martingales attach to the reins, while standing martingales are fixed to the back of the nose band. Neither type should hold the horse's head down – and both should come into play only when the horse's head is too high for rider comfort and control.

The two reins are attached to the bit rings and are joined together with a buckle near the rider's hands. They can be plain leather, plaited leather, leather with rubber for extra grip or webbing. Western reins are separate pieces, called split reins, and they can be made of a variety of materials, including mohair rope, nylon rope and plaited parachute cord.

Cleaning your tack regularly allows you a chance to inspect it for wear. Of course you should repair or replace anything that is about to break, and keep a close eye on anything that is heavily worn. Good-quality horse tack is made to hold up to the job it is made to do, and keeping it clean will help it hold up that much longer.

Cleaning Leather Tack

To clean leather, you will need a good sponge, warm water, your favourite leather cleaning product (commonly called saddle soap), and a bottle of your favourite leather conditioner. Undo any straps, remove the girth from your saddle, and unbuckle any pieces that buckle on and off so that you can be sure to get into every little nook and cranny where dirt loves to hide and grind at the leather. Wash everything down with warm water and the sponge, opening up the pores of the leather. Use some elbow grease to remove any surface dirt. Rinse off, get some clean warm water, dab some leather cleaner onto the sponge and lather up your leather. Rinse it off and let it dry a bit. Before it is completely dry, work in some leather conditioner. Bear in mind that some leather conditioners may darken light leather, so test a hidden area first before doing the entire piece.

Keep your leather tack – saddles, bridles and leather halters – in a cool, dry place. Dampness will cause mould to form on the leather, and too much heat and sun exposure will dry it out.

Horsewear

Leg Protection

Boots on the horse are used for protection either from external injury – usually the horse striking one leg with another foot – or from striking a rail when jumping or rocks and fallen branches on a hack. Learn to put them on snugly, but not so tightly as to cut off circulation. There are several different kinds of boots.

- **Travelling boots:** these padded wraps are used for all four legs during transporting. They often have a fleecy lining and are done up with Velcro straps.
- **Bell boots:** these boots are basically rubber boots (they also come in synthetic materials such as Cordura) that look like the business end of a sink plunger and hang from the horse's fetlock joint.
- **Brushing boots:** this protection is for the lower front leg area, both from striking it with the other foot or from the concussion of hard or deep, heavy footing. These wrap around the leg between the knee and the fetlock and have Velcro closures.
- **Tendon or galloping boots:** usually made of leather or neoprene, these boots protect the back of the horse's front legs/feet from overreaching with the back legs at the gallop.
- **Open front or tendon boots:** more boots used in jumping, these are for the front legs and are open in the front.

Rugs

The following are the basic types of rugs available:

- **Fly sheet:** this is a thin mesh sheet that is cool in warm weather but protects the horse's body from biting flies.
- **Anti-sweat sheet:** this is a lightweight sheet used for cooling out a sweaty horse.
- **Cooler:** traditionally wool, but also synthetic or cotton, this light rug traps air while the horse cools off, and provides some warmth once the horse has cooled.
- **Rain sheets:** made of waterproof material, these sheets are also made big enough to cover a saddle while you're waiting for your class.
- **Summer sheet:** this provides some warmth and protection from wind.
- **Turnout rug:** this has a thermal duvet-like filling and a strong waterproof outer to provide protection from the weather.
- **Exercise sheet:** worn while riding, this rug fits under the saddle and covers the rump, keeping the loin area warm during warm-up.
- **Stable rug:** this is usually quilted and is put on in the stable to keep the horse warm, but the rug is not waterproof.

Equipment and Clothing for the Rider

Hats

The most important thing about the hat or helmet you pick is its size. It should fit snugly on your head, and should be buckled under your chin before you mount up. All hats, helmets and riding skulls should conform to current safety standards, such as BSEN1384, PAS015 or ASTM F116/SE1, which show that they offer a minimum quality of protection. Most riding establishments and horse shows require hats of these standards to be worn.

In the USA, where riding hats are not so widely worn as in Britain, head injuries account for the largest percentage of all serious injuries resulting from horse-riding accidents. Buy a helmet that fits well, and always wear it when you ride.

Helmets come in all sorts of styles, and even a few colours these days. There are different designs that are considered more appropriate than others for different types of riding. The velvet kind with the little button on the top is most common in the show ring. Schooling helmets tend to have a lot of open ventilation. You can accessorize your helmet with decorative helmet covers and rain covers.

Body Protectors

Although not many recreational riders wear body protectors, if you plan to do a lot of jumping or start a lot of young horses under saddle, protectors are a worthwhile investment. As with hats, body protectors are available that should meet basic safety standards (there are several levels; ask your tack supplier to explain them to you). They are very lightweight and have lots of features to make them more comfortable than ever. Most cost up to £120, although there are some that are more expensive.

There are lots of mail-order catalogues that offer a wide range of riding clothes at reasonable prices. It is also worth having a look through horse magazines, as they often ask riders to test out various items and then rate them according to the results.

Clothing and Footwear

Jodhpurs

English riders and riding breeches are extremely comfortable and come in stretch fabrics that are intended to fit very tightly. Many have suede or faux-suede patches inside the knees. You can also get full-seat breeches where the suede runs from the knee of one leg all the way around the bottom, and back down to the knee of the other leg; not only do these wear better, but the full suede seat helps to keep your seat in the saddle.

Chaps

One way to save wear and tear on your jodhpurs is to wear chaps. These can be leather or suede or a synthetic material, and may or may not have a fringe. They are made to zip on the outside and fit quite snugly to your leg. Chaps may cover the whole leg – full chaps – or come up to the knee – half chaps.

Boots

There are two basic types of riding boots – long boots (up to your knees) and jodhpur boots (up to your ankles). There are also various waterproof wellington boots and mucker boots that are not suitable for riding but excellent for use around the yard. Both long boots and jodhpur boots are acceptable in competitions and for general hacking, although in practice long boots are more often worn in competitions nowadays. There is a huge choice of boots, and the best advice is to try some out and see what suits you best. If you choose jodhpur boots, you'll probably want half chaps as well for general riding.

Whatever type of boot you go for, make sure that it has a significant heel to prevent your foot from slipping completely through the stirrup. It is also a good idea to have some toe protection.

> Boots for riding have a completely different purpose than boots for yard work. Sturdy boots are a must, and you'll definitely want a waterproof pair around. In winter, you'll also need a pair of warm boots. Manure and urine take a toll on leather and rubber, so expect to have to replace your boots at least every couple of years.

Spurs

As with dressage whips and riding crops, spurs should be considered a means of supporting your leg but used only as incentive, never as punishment. The most common spurs worn by most riders have very short shanks.

Find a Style That's Right for You

This is just an overview of the equipment for horse and rider that is needed and is available, but it will get you started. Once you begin to look through catalogues and tack shops, you will get a sense of what styles are right for you. Keep in mind that there is a range of prices that suits every budget. The most important thing is comfort; don't give up comfort for the sake of fashion. And if the price of something – a bit, a device, a piece of equipment – seems too good to be true, it is. Don't waste your money on it. Buy the simplest equipment of the best quality that you can afford.

CHAPTER 14

Riding and Driving

Although horse owners take great pleasure in caring for their horses, riding is still typically the ultimate intent. It's fun, challenging, interesting and good exercise, all wrapped into one.

There's a lot you can learn from reading, but let me say up front that you will not learn how to ride from a book or a video. The real place to learn to ride is on a horse. If all you ever did was ride – if you never picked up a book, watched a video or had a lesson – you could still become a fantastic rider, but you need to learn how to learn from your horse. An instructor helping you get started is probably a good way to learn to be in the saddle in a way that helps the horse instead of hindering him. But often good riding boils down to time in the saddle.

Develop Your Awareness

A little common sense and awareness will take you a long way. In order for a horse to be comfortable carrying your extra weight, you need to learn to be balanced in your seat so that you aren't using your horse's mouth for balance, and you need to learn not to flop around in the saddle. If you become aware of how the horse is responding to what you do, you will be able to adjust what you are doing to fit the horse.

Be Particular About Who You Learn From

I get very frustrated watching videos and competitions in which people who are either instructing others or are considered the top competitors in their discipline have horses that are foaming at the mouth (some say that this is an indication of something good, but I don't agree) and are kept under control only by an iron grip on the reins. Don't aspire to that. While they are claiming that having every part of their body in the exact right position is best for the horse, their horses are there in living colour showing the opposite. Pick your teachers carefully.

When I got back into horses after a decade of not riding, I realized I should take some lessons. But I needed more saddle time than during the weekly lesson. A friend offered to let me ride her older mare during the week when she couldn't get to the yard. This helped keep her mare exercised, and gave me riding time on a solid horse.

Do aspire to be a relaxed rider who can instill calmness in your horse. Even if all the technical details aren't perfect and every inch of your body isn't where the 'professionals' say it should be, it is much better to be a relaxed horse and rider.

Learning How to Ride

If you've never ridden a horse before, probably the best place to have your first ride is at a reputable riding stables that teach beginners the fundamentals. Not only will they have horses and instructors, but they will have saddles and hats for students to use, and you won't have to spend a lot of money before you've even sat on a horse. However, do have a pair of sturdy boots, even if they aren't 'riding' boots. For safety, the boots should have at least a 12mm (^{1}/$_2$in) heel, then, in the event of your being thrown from your horse, your boot won't go through the stirrup and trap your foot.

How to Find a Good Riding Stable

The Yellow Pages are a starting place for collecting locations – look under Riding Schools. You should do some investigating and asking around before signing up for lessons.

Another place to look is on the bulletin board at local tack shops and feed stores for flyers from local stables offering lessons. As you investigate, ask the staff at the shop whether they know anything about the stable.

Once you've collected names, you can start with a phone call. Talk to the stable manager, who may or may not be one of the instructors, about what is offered, asking questions such as these:

- *What kind of riding lessons does the school offer? Is there a concentration on any one discipline?* If you just want to have a few lessons to get on a horse and start to develop your ability, it may not matter what the stable's focus is at first. But if you end up wanting to continue and the place you started with doesn't offer what you're interested in, you will have to change schools. That may not be an issue, but it would be best to find somewhere that has at least some range of disciplines. It's hard enough to find a place in which you feel comfortable, without having to change not long after you start.
- *Are both private and group lessons available?* Some beginning riders may want to start with private lessons until they develop their seat, and then after a few weeks, when they are more comfortable, they can join a group lesson to learn how to ride with other horses and riders around. Some people prefer just the opposite – to ride with a group for the moral support while learning, then develop and refine their skills with private lessons.
- *What should I bring with me to the lesson?* The stable is likely to provide everything you need, but don't assume anything. Find out whether you

need your own hat. Even if they do provide one, having your own personal hat that fits you correctly is best. If you decide that horse riding isn't for you, a hat will be easy enough to sell.

When you start looking for a riding school, you will come across some that are BHS Approved. The British Horse Society started 'approving' schools in 1961, and those that are approved will meet certain standards in horse welfare, safety considerations and instruction. The BHS website (*www.bhs.org.uk*) has a list of all their approved schools and a key to tell you what is offered in the way of teaching, hacking and riding holidays. The Association of British Riding Schools (*www.abrs.org.uk*) can also recommend riding schools.

- *Do they have lesson horses available?* Again, any stable that spends a lot of time on giving lessons probably has lesson horses on the premises, but don't take that for granted. Ask what the horses are like, too.
- *Can I eventually take lessons on my own horse?* Maybe you already own a horse but would like to learn on a lesson horse first, then switch to your own. Find out if they are comfortable with this idea.
- *May I come and watch a lesson?* This may be your most important question of all. My personal view is that if a school is uncomfortable with you coming and watching what takes place there, then maybe you won't be comfortable with what takes place there. Granted, the instructor should always ask the student who is having a lesson if it is OK if a prospective student watches. Otherwise, however, dropping in on a facility that you'd like to develop a relationship with should not be a big issue.

Finding an Instructor

This is where some self-analysis will come in. People teach and people learn in myriad ways. If an instructor has a drill-sergeant approach, barking out orders and screaming at you, telling you how stupid you are every time you do something wrong, and you have the tendency to crawl inside yourself whenever you get yelled at, this is not the right instructor or approach for you. Some people get a lot out of this 'tough love' kind of instruction – the more they are yelled at, the more they are challenged to perfect what they are doing.

Other people need to be constantly reassured and encouraged. This may sound like the ideal approach, but actually this can go too far as well. You want to be praised for your accomplishments, but if you want to become a good and better rider, you also need some constructive criticism.

Somewhere in between is probably best for most people, especially the beginning rider. Praise for what you are doing right, while being made aware of where you need to adjust and improve, can move you along from the beginner to the advanced beginner stages quickly.

You might enjoy browsing through *www.horseandhound.co.uk*, which is in an online magazine format and has articles about riding and show results from around the country.

You can learn something about how an instructor teaches by watching him or her give a lesson. But this can be a bit misleading, since the instructor knows you are watching and evaluating. The best test of an instructor is to take one or two lessons – a good school will even suggest that. Don't sign up for a series of lessons; just pay for them as you go. If the first one goes well, pay for another. Do this three or four times, and if the relationship continues to go well and there is a financial incentive to buy a few lessons at once or in joining a group lesson of a series of six lessons for a set fee, then you can feel comfortable doing that. If the first couple of lessons do not go well or you just aren't sure, try out other instructors until you find your match.

The 'Lesson' Horse

A riding stable that concentrates on giving lessons will have 'lesson' horses – usually well-trained horses, probably in their teens, that have had a lot of exposure to the outside world. They tend to be calm and cool about being ridden, and are also very tolerant of riders of different skill levels.

The horses themselves will tell you a lot about the overall quality of the stables and the experience you will have taking lessons there. Do the horses seem content? One of the most obvious things you can judge is how well they are cared for – 'lesson' horses can work pretty hard, which means they should be fit and trim, but not skinny. Are their coats shiny, appropriately long or short, depending on the time of year? Are their feet well cared for? Do you see lame horses being ridden for lessons?

Lessons on Your Own Horse

If you own your own horse, you may have it in mind to eventually use your horse for your lessons. Depending on the horse, the beginning rider may find it best to take a few lessons on the stable's horses in order to advance his or her skills on horses that know the drill. Once you have perfected the basics, you can switch to your own horse with confidence.

The hardest part about taking lessons on your own horse is that you may have a specific way of doing things with your horse and your instructor may do things differently. If that is the case, you need to find a middle ground. Also, you want your horse's education to be advanced enough for you to be able to concentrate on your lesson, not on trying to control your horse.

Clinics

Over the past few years, the clinic scene has really taken off. These learning environments usually offer the opportunity to be a spectator or bring your horse and participate as a student. With clinics, the human is the student, and the horse is the project.

As an older rider re-introducing myself to horsemanship, I embraced clinics as a way to learn, especially about handling and working with young horses. Most areas of the country offer clinics somewhere within easy travelling distance, as trainers tend to travel all over the country for most of the year.

If you are experiencing problems with a horse or want to improve your riding so that you can be more comfortable with your horse, clinics are a great place to spend an intensive amount of time. You and your horse will develop a stronger relationship just by learning together under good instruction. The clinic environment provides instant cameraderie and instant access to a teacher.

Getting the Most Out of Attending a Clinic

I have been to literally dozens of clinics given by several different trainers in many different disciplines over the past decade, some as a spectator and some as a participant. In my experience, these are the things you need to consider in order to get the most out of your time and money, both of which can be considerable.

- *Check the trainers before you sign up to participate.* The best way to do this is to be a spectator. If a trainer is coming to a place near you, find his or her schedule and see where else he or she is giving a clinic. Maybe you can combine a short holiday with a trip to the clinic in another area. This is a great way to meet horse people in other parts of the country, and you can observe the trainer before signing up for the clinic near you. Many trainers also offer videos, but the best way to check their style is to watch them in person.
- *Find out everything you need to have for the clinic for both you and your horse.* To participate in a general horsemanship clinic, you usually need whatever you normally ride in. Horsemanship clinics are sometimes offered in specific disciplines, such as jumping or dressage; you will need your usual equipment to perform in that discipline. But beyond that, do you need shavings? Buckets? Muck bucket and manure fork? Organizers usually send out information sheets along with release forms; if you have any questions that are still unanswered, phone and ask. You don't want to lessen your experience by being unprepared.
- *Be willing to try new things.* The trainer will have ideas about exercises and activities that work to teach certain things. You are there to learn, so join in and fully participate.

Clinics and demonstrations are often held by well-known horsemen and women, but they can also be held by local horsey people. Each of these will have something to teach you, and it is worth attending any that you think sound interesting, not just those held by the famous. Look in horse magazines and check the bulletin boards at your local tack shop to find out what's going on in your area.

- *Don't spend your time making excuses for your horse or your riding.* If your horse is being a fool, spend your time learning how to help your horse not act like a fool. Your riding level isn't an issue – you are there to learn! If the clinic offers a couple of different classes, make sure you sign up for the class that is most appropriate for your level of experience. You have the perfect opportunity to change things under the direction of a very knowledgeable person, so make use of it. A clinic is not a horse show where you are showing off what you and your horse know. It is a learning experience.
- *Watch everything.* Turn up early to take care of your horse, and be ready for the first class, whether or not you are in it. Some things that are going on may not look like they have anything to do with you and your horse, but you would be surprised how much you can learn from something that seems completely unrelated. Participate fully in the clinic. Even lunch can be a learning experience.
- *Ask questions.* Participation in a clinic can be expensive. Sometimes even spectator fees are substantial. Feel free to ask questions, even if they seem stupid. A good trainer will be happy to answer questions – in fact, they often seem to wish people would ask more questions!

Moving On

The things you learn at a clinic should give you the knowledge and comfort level you need to move out into the real world with your horse. Clinics are safe environments in which to try things under controlled circumstances with knowledgeable help at your fingertips.

It can be disconcerting to ride with people who haven't learned to do things in the same way that you have. But you will begin to appreciate how much you and your horse have learned when you ride outside the clinic environment and your education and the education you are providing your horse all hangs together.

Fitness

Both you and your horse need to be physically fit to be comfortable for any length of time in the saddle. The overweight, unfit horse will quickly get winded and sweaty. She will also get saddle sores, girth galls and other soreness related to carrying around too much weight, as well as being prone to injury and illness. You need to be fit enough to use your body to request your horse to do what you ask – this doesn't mean that horseback riders need to be supermodel-thin, of course, but riding horses is a physical activity that requires some level of fitness and flexibility, no matter what your size.

Fitness of the Horse

Prepare your horse for the level of riding you plan to use him for. If you take him out just on weekends for a hack a couple of miles long, he can probably be a little overweight and out of shape and deal with it. But don't expect that same horse to go out one weekend on a 25-mile pleasure ride. He will be sore; it is probable that he will damage something, making him unrideable for a few weeks; and it just isn't fair. Condition your horse for the amount of riding you plan to do. If you want to do that 25-mile ride, plan ahead for it.

If your horse has been resting for a while for whatever reason – perhaps you can't ride much during winter when it gets dark before you get home from work – make sure you give her time to get fit again before asking too much of her. This may involve a few weeks of walking-only rides, building up to a few short trots, before you bring in canter and she is up to a good level of fitness again.

Fitness of the Rider

Being around horses will bring you some innate strength training just from day-to-day chores such as lifting water buckets, food bags, bags of shavings and so on. But there are some things to add to your overall fitness regimen that can be helpful, specifically for riding.

Stretching is very important. Add some good yoga and stretching books to your library and pick out some exercises. Of course, as with any physical activity, you should do some basic stretches before you get on your horse. But also some more in-depth stretching is good – perhaps some yoga poses. You will be able to get on and off your horse more easily, your muscles won't be as sore from the stretching they get from simply being astride a horse, and if the horse spooks and stretches your muscles even further, they won't be starting from such a tight place. Your horse will move better and respond to your body better if you are more supple. And you will be able to move with the horse better and boost the energy that you need to transfer energy to her.

Your lower back absorbs a lot of the shock of the motion of riding. A strong back and correspondingly strong abdominal muscles will help keep this shock absorption from making your back hurt. Strong abdominal muscles will also help your posture in the saddle. So add abdominal stomach crunches to your exercise programme!

What are psychocybernetics?
This is the technique for using your subconscious power to achieve the positive results that you desire. In *That Winning Feeling?* Jane Savoie talks about this concept in relation to horses and riding.

How to Ride

Explaining how to ride a horse in a book is a tall order. But there are a few basic things to know that you will run into the first time you climb on board a horse.

The Paces

The horse has three basic paces that the beginner will encounter and want to master:

1. **The walk:** the horse walks with three feet on the ground and one foot raised at any one time. Each hoof strikes the ground individually – one, two, three, four.
2. **The trot:** this is a two-beat pace; two feet are on the ground and two feet are in the air at any one time. The feet operate on a diagonal pattern, with the left front and right hind either up or down at the same time, and the same with the right front and left hind, with a brief moment when all four feet are off the ground.
3. **The canter:** this is a three-beat gait with a hind leg pushing off, then the other hind and the opposite front, then the other front leg, with a moment of complete suspension when all four legs are off the ground.

FIGURE 14.1:
Foot patterns

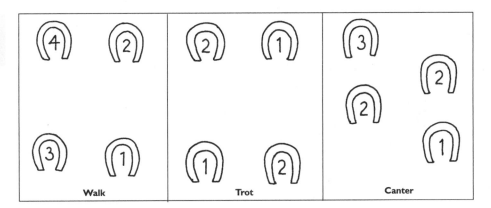

Riding the Three Paces

- **The walk:** sit deeply in the saddle and move your body with the movement of the horse. Expect the horse to walk with energy and life; none of this dull, slow walking. You should both look as if you are enjoying yourself and have somewhere to go. At first, your body movements may be a bit exaggerated, but you will learn to have life in your body without swinging like a monkey up there.

- **The trot:** at some point, you will want to learn to 'sit the trot', using your lower back to absorb the shock of the up-and-down movement, and not flop around like a dying fish in the saddle. However, you will probably also want to do a rising trot, also known as posting. You rise out of the saddle with the rise of the outside (the one along the fence rail or arena wall) front foot, and you sit back into the saddle as that outside front foot falls to the ground. Rising trot is easier if the horse is trotting with some speed. And don't fret if you don't get it at first – once you get the rhythm, it will be like riding a bicycle and will never leave you. This is where a good school horse helps, because it knows to keep the trot pace up, even though what you may be doing with your body interferes with its ability to move.
- **The canter:** in general, the canter is a pace with which beginners are very uncomfortable. This is, I think, mostly because of the additional speed with which the horse is moving. If you can find a smooth reliable horse to learn to canter on from the very beginning, you will save yourself a lot of canter angst and master this pace early in your riding career. This can be truly that proverbial rocking horse feeling. You need to learn to sit up straight to keep your weight balanced and in your stirrups, and to scoop your seat along with the movement of the saddle/the horse's back. Sometimes a novice rider has trouble getting a horse to canter at all – their anxiety makes their body block the horse from moving. As with anything involving horses, the more you canter in a controlled environment, the sooner you will be comfortable.

To learn a specific discipline, look for an instructor in that discipline. He or she will be able to teach you what kind of tack you will need, how to ride in the proper position, what to wear if you plan to compete, and the etiquette of competition for that discipline.

The most important thing is to start with the basics of riding – the things that are universal, no matter what discipline you plan to ride or what type of equipment you plan to use. Listed opposite are some of the most important basic things to master in order to ride well.

·   *Be calm.* Your calmness will help your horse to be calm. Horses very often take after their owners – a nervous person will make a horse nervous too, and a laid-back person will tend to bring out the laid-back part of a horse. The more calm you are on top of your horse, the better. If you take lessons, your instructor will probably tell you a million times to breathe. Holding your breath or taking shallow short breaths has an effect not only on you but also on your horse. Keep in mind that the horse can feel a fly land on any part of its body – imagine how much it can feel what you are doing up there!

·   *Learn about how your horse perceives things, and try to assess a situation from her perspective.* A horse does not think like a human; it's as simple as that. The advantage we humans have is that we can analyze our own behaviour and the behaviour of others. Use that ability, and learn about how the horse thinks. Your horse *does* think, every second of the day! Horses are not stupid; they just think like horses. This isn't to say you should spend your time second-guessing them. But if you come upon a trouble spot with your horse, put yourself in your horse's shoes and think about how she might be perceiving the situation. Lots of research has been done here, so there's plenty of information to read. And there's always the best teacher of all – your horse – to learn from.

·   *Sit on your horse as if your intention is to be there.* Don't slouch like a sack of potatoes and expect your horse to react positively to what you ask of him. Similarly, don't sit as stiff as a board. Move with the horse and exhibit energy when you want your horse to exhibit energy. Instructors will tell you to hold your shoulders exactly in this position and your legs in exactly that position and to hold your reins this or that way and tilt your wrists at this or that angle, but not too far. Relax! Hold yourself on your horse in a warm, inviting way in a position that is conducive to riding with purpose.

·   *Do what you are ready for.* This isn't to say you shouldn't push yourself, but also keep in mind that the only timeline you have is self-inflicted. Your horse couldn't care less if the two of you progress beyond a certain level in a sport. Don't step up to the canter out on a hack if you don't think either of you are ready for it. Do what you are ready for, and work on preparing to be ready for more.

- *Avoid gimmicks.* If a piece of tack or a training device claims to work miracles, don't buy it. Becoming a good rider that a horse can rely on for moral support is hard work, and you should plan to work hard to become the team you can be proud of. If you don't enjoy hard work, you should think about taking up a different hobby.
- *Don't drill your horse.* Yes, you will need to do things enough times that the horse learns it, but don't spend all evening working on one thing. Mix it up for the horse. Give your horse the benefit of being the thinking, reasoning animal she is, and give her some variety. Add exterior stimuli to your riding sessions – you'd be amazed how much a few trotting poles, low jumps, tarpaulins, gates to go through or even a couple of cows can add to your horse's interest level.

It's just not worth risking your safety or that of your horse to attempt something that gives you pause, such as crossing a questionable wooden bridge or riding across that road instead of getting off and leading your horse across. It is your responsibility to keep your team as safe as possible.

Here are some additional basic riding elements:

- **Upwards/downwards transitions:** when a horse changes pace, it is known as a transition. An upwards transition is from a slower pace to a faster pace. A downwards transition is from a faster pace to a slower pace. You need to help your horse make these transitions smoothly and upon request by learning to ride the changes smoothly yourself and knowing how to ask the horse to change from one pace to the other.
- **Counter canter:** a horse canters on a specific lead when going in a circle. The lead is determined by the back inside leg, which provides balance and support to the inside of the circle. The horse cantering in a circle to the left should be on a 'left lead'. A counter canter is cantering using the opposite lead from the one that would be appropriate for the direction the horse is going. A counter canter is sometimes used intentionally for conditioning and strengthening.

- **Flexion and bend:** flexion is the vertical – back-to-front and up-and-down – flexibility of the horse, while bend is the side-to-side flexibility of the horse. These terms can sometimes be interchangeable.
- **Lateral movement:** this refers to the sideways movements of the horse.
- **Working on a line:** As you ride, you want to have an imaginary line out ahead of you that you aim to stay on. This is most evident in jumping, where before the horse and rider have finished sailing over one jump, the rider is already looking toward the next jump and aiming the horse along the imaginary line he or she has determined to get to the exact position they want to be in when they get to the jump.

Some Things You Want From Your Horse

To be safe riding, there are a few things I have learned to expect from my horses. These are things that make me feel safe when riding. Riding a horse is fraught with danger – but if I have these things at my disposal, I feel comfortable about being able to work through almost any situation, and I feel more in control. I work towards refining the following things.

Constantly kicking with your legs or tapping with a crop can make your horse dull. If you need to go to this step, make absolutely sure that you get the energy you expect from your horse so that the action remains effective.

Responsiveness

You want your horse to be responsive when you ask her to do something. If you pick up the reins, you want her to come to attention and go through with whatever you ask her to do. It is up to you to help her understand what you are asking, but you need to expect responsiveness. If you don't expect your horse to be responsive, you teach her that you don't really mean what you ask. And sometimes when you ask for something, it is a matter of safety that your horse is responsive – such as stopping to avoid a kick from the horse ahead, or moving one foot to the left to avoid falling into a ditch.

There are three stages in asking your horse to do something. The first is the 'energy in your body' stage. If you bring up the energy by lifting your weight out of your seat and preparing to move with the movement of the horse, your horse will bring up her energy too. That energy will exhibit itself in whatever you are asking of her – if you have contact with the bit blocking forward movement, she will move that energy backwards; if you bring up energy without contact, she will move forwards.

If your energy means nothing to the horse, you need to go to the next stage, which is the 'squeeze with your legs for forward movement' stage.

If this does nothing, you need to follow through with step three, which is the 'whatever it takes' step. Tap the horse with the end of your rein, or use a dressage whip or crop to encourage the horse. This is a last resort step, and you should work with your horse in order to avoid it.

Softness

When you pick up the reins, you want your horse to melt into your hands. Picking up those reins is a signal to your horse that you are about to work at something. This doesn't mean you have to have strong contact with the horse's mouth, but you should expect your horse to be alert to what you have in mind for the two of you. Softness means that when you pick up the reins the horse doesn't resist against you, throwing his head up in the air. If an emergency should come up, you want softness, not resistance, to be your horse's first response to you.

Say you are in a pack of horses riding along a track and something spooks the group, such as a bird flying out of the bushes. There's a pretty good chance that your horse will spook with the rest – it's only natural. Would you really want your horse to be so dull and sour about life as to not have some reaction to this kind of thing? But what you want next is for the horse to turn to you for a message about the situation. If you pick up the reins and your horse softens, the situation for the two of you will go from potentially explosive to controlled. If the horse's first reaction is to resist your hands and throw his head up in the air, the situation is going to get more frightening.

Move the Hindquarters Away

When I first ride a young horse, I spend a lot of time asking that horse to bring its head around towards my leg. To do this, I shorten the rein by bringing it back towards my hip on the side I want the horse to bend towards, and completely release the rein on the other side to give the horse the room to bend.

Once the horse is readily giving her head, it's time to add on to that by asking with the leg on the same side for the horse to step its hindquarters away. This move takes a lot of work from the ground first (see Chapter 11). It will come in handy in many ways. First, it seems to be very relaxing to the horse, perhaps because it gives the horse something to think about – something relatively easy.

Modified versions of this move can be used for many things, including stepping around an object, opening a gate and even using up some excess energy on a hack (if your horse is a little too eager, pick up one rein and use the leg on the same side to get her doing loops from one side of the track to the other). You should also guide the front quarters at this point (guide her rear around one leg and her front over with the other).

Backing

Don't satisfy yourself with a pathetic little step backwards and think that's backing. Expect your horse to back up for as long as you are asking him to, and with as much energy as you are asking for. When you are first teaching him to back, pick up the reins, get softness and bending at the poll from your horse, shift your weight back a little, and when he backs even one step, release all pressure – reins, weight, energy. Build on that, asking for more steps as he begins to understand what you want. By the time he really knows how to back, he should back to the next county if you haven't released him yet.

A horse backs up in the same diagonal pattern as the trot – with a hind foot and its opposite front foot off the ground at the same time.

You can put some of these pieces together and back in circles. This is a lot more complicated than it sounds! Your horse's head will be a little to the outside of the circle, enough to just see his eye on that side. Ask for your back, and guide your horse's hindquarters with your outside leg to move slightly to the inside, and his front quarters with your inside leg to move slightly to the outside as you are backing. If you ask too much with either leg, you won't have a circle at all; your horse will step over behind or across in front in place. If you don't ask for enough energy while backing, you will not get the circle either. It's a great exercise, but it can be frustrating for both of you. Satisfy yourself with perhaps a quarter of a circle for a few times, then half the circle, and build up to the full circle. Your horse's hoof prints in the dirt will show you whether you've made a circle, an oval or just muddled around!

Falling Off

It happens. For a while when first starting to ride my gelding, and not having been in the saddle for years, I was falling off once or twice each session. Not having ridden for a while, I was particularly easy to unseat; it would take very little in the way of a buck or twist or quick turn to find me sailing through the air. You probably won't repeat my experience, but the chances are that you will fall off once in a while.

It is important to get back on if you want to continue horse riding as a pastime, but falling can make you very fearful. Don't just put it down to life in the horse lane. Think about why your horse spooked, bucked, reared or did whatever it did to send you flying. Go back to refining those tools mentioned earlier – maybe the next time the horse bolts, you can regain control, help him calm down and settle the scene before he bucks or you lose your balance. A horse occasionally spooking is a fact of life – regaining control and defusing the situation as quickly as possible is the key to avoiding the bucks and bolts, and the potential fall. Work on your balance – this can be one of the most important things that can help you remain seated.

Driving

Although not as common as riding, driving is good fun and quite a challenge. If you plan to get into driving intensively, you should find a place to take some lessons and perhaps partner someone more experienced for a while. One way to find someone like this is to attend a nearby horse show that includes driving classes.

If you want to drive your horse just for fun, the same approach applies to driving as riding: don't surprise your horse, but expose her deliberately to things. If you ride your horse, you won't need to expose her to the driving bridle; she will be accustomed to having a bridle on. But here are some things to keep in mind as you begin to harness her:

·   Get her accustomed to having things dangling around her legs and off her body. You can do this with lots of things in a 'sacking out' kind of approach, not just with the harness itself. Start with dangling the lead rope around her legs, use the flag talked about in the handling chapter, maybe even work up to using a small tarpaulin. Make sure she's happy with all this before hooking all the buckles and straps on the harness and having her freak out.

·   Put the harness on one piece at a time. This may mean taking the harness apart a bit more than normal, but it's worth it. When she is fully comfortable with one section of the harness, get her accustomed to the next, until she's got the whole thing on.

·   Get help in finding the most appropriate vehicle for your horse. Make sure you feel your horse is thoroughly exposed to the driving reins before strapping a cart behind her. It will pay to get her to learn to pull something simple, such as a progression of heavier logs, before hitching her up.

Driving has a wealth of intricacies to learn. Read some of the books in Appendix A and, most importantly, find an experienced person from whom you can learn.

Riding Experiences Differ

Riding horses is a different experience for everyone. Some people seem to be natural riders with great flexibility and no fear; others have to work very hard to be balanced and at ease on the back of a horse. But once you get the hang of it, you will join the large group of people who have rear-window stickers and T-shirts that say 'I'd rather be riding'.

CHAPTER 15

Equine Careers

A career involving equines can take many avenues. Some are obvious – veterinarian or farrier – but with the current explosion of the horse industry, the career path one can take is wide open. If you love horses so much that you'd like to make them your life's work, this chapter is for you.

One thing to keep in mind is that no matter what path you might take in making horses the focus of your career, if you plan to open your own business – whether it is a veterinary practice or a tack shop – you will need to fit some business courses in around the equine studies: all businesses have some basic elements that increase the chances for survival.

Equine Veterinarian

An equine veterinarian career can take a couple of paths. You can either have your own practice or join an established practice. You can specialize in large animals or be a general large/small animal veterinarian. Some people like working with a variety of animals, including dogs, cats, goats, sheep and ferrets, as well as equines; some prefer to stick with just equines.

As with human medicine, extensive time in university is required to be a veterinarian. As you progress in your education, you may begin to hone in on a speciality that you find yourself attracted to – for example, surgery, therapeutics or research. Write to veterinary schools to learn more about the level of schooling required and the areas of expertise available to you from veterinary schools around the country.

Pets, including horses, are a vital part of the economy in the United Kingdom and developed nations around the world. Veterinarians can make a good living. Most horse veterinarians are on the road a lot, so you need to like to drive, be able to find your way through country towns and roads, and improvise with whatever kind of facility you find at the end of the road. There are equine hospitals, where you might be able to stay put, but they are few and far between.

Only six universities currently offer veterinary training, so competition for places is fierce and you have to have good exam results to get in, as well as being able to show commitment to the training. Universities offering training are Bristol, Cambridge, Edinburgh, Glasgow, Liverpool and London. For more information about applying to university, write to The Secretary, UCAS, Fulton House, Jessop Avenue, Cheltenham, Gloucestershire GL50 3SH.

Veterinary Nurse

The veterinary nurse is a vital part of an animal hospital of any kind. Nurses in equine practices may find themselves doing anything from cleaning stables to taking temperatures to regularly checking in-house patients for vital signs, changing bandages, restocking vets' vehicles or answering the phones. Some nurses go on the road with vets and help prepare vaccines, hold horses while care is being administered and so forth. For more information about veterinary nursing, contact the British Veterinary Nursing Association (BVNA), Level 15, Terminus House, Terminus Street, Harlow, Essex CM20 1XA.

Equine Dentist

Veterinarians do not tend to get intensive training in any one area, so the equine dentist is becoming a more common member of the horse care team. Keep in mind that you will spend a lot of time with your hands in a horse's mouth, and unless you can get yourself a few customers who have large facilities with lots of horses, you will also, like a vet, need to travel around the countryside to your customers.

The tools needed for dentistry are minimal, although you can choose between simple hand tools or more expensive power tools that take the strain off your back and shoulders. This can be tiring but fascinating work, and it is a thriving profession.

Farrier

Let me say up front that farrier work can be hard on the body. If all horses were easy to handle, stood perfectly still for the farrier and held their own weight up while the farrier worked on a foot, then maybe it would be less of a backbreaking job. But those kinds of horses are more the rarity than the norm, so be prepared for hard physical work.

What's the difference between a farrier and a blacksmith?
A **farrier** is a blacksmith who does horseshoeing but doesn't necessarily do other types of iron work. A **blacksmith** is not a horseshoer but someone who makes things with iron.

The horse's foot is fascinating, and its well-being is vital to the overall well-being of the horse. The tools needed for farrier work are fairly simple, the work is varied and you are your own boss. Like the country vet, you have to travel around the countryside and deal with whatever set-ups you come across. The farrier also often works in conjunction with the veterinarian for foot issues that involve disease and injury.

You should find a farrier to whom you can be apprenticed. You will learn from him or her, and will also attend regular college training sessions of anything from a few days to a few weeks. The area of foot care is always changing, with new techniques and shoes made of new materials, and the need for people in this area of equine speciality is increasing.

For more information, contact the Farrier Training Service, Sefton House, Adam Court, Newark Road, Peterborough PE1 5PP.

Saddler

You can train to make saddles or to fit them, or both. You can either do this through a college course or by becoming an apprentice to a master saddler. You will also be in demand for reflocking saddles and mending other items of tack, such as reins or driving harness. For more information, contact the Society of Master Saddlers (UK) Limited, Kettles Farm, Mickfield, Stowmarket, Suffolk IP14 6BY.

Holistic Practitioner

Holistic horse health is of great interest to horse owners these days. If you enjoy the health aspect of the equine industry and like to get your hands on horses, you can become a massage therapist or chiropractor, both of which are in demand, especially in the performance world but also increasingly by the everyday horse owner. Skills in Reiki, acupuncture and acupressure are all becoming ways to earn money working with horses. (See Chapter 10 for more on holistic approaches.)

Livery Yard Owner/Manager

In order to own or manage a livery yard, you will need either years of experience or an equine management degree. You will also need superb people skills! Managing a livery yard can be the best of both worlds. There are often some perks that go with the deal that need to be considered as part of the salary package. These can be in the form of a stable or two for your own horse(s), a place to live on the premises and free admission to any events that take place at the livery yard. You can often feed your own horses cheaply, since you will be buying feed in bulk for the yard, and there are other smaller hidden savings.

Running a livery yard requires a lot of diversity. You will be arranging for building and equipment repairs, dealing with feed suppliers, maintaining the surface of the arena, handling all kinds of horses – the list is endless. It can be challenging and rewarding to run a top-notch livery yard that is teeming with business – but don't expect much of a private life!

Equine Lawyer

The proverbial 'litigious society' is quick to extend that tendency to the horse world. If law interests you and you are thinking of studying law, you can begin to work on an expertise in equine law from your personal horse experience. People have sued over unbelievable equine-related things – you will never lack for variety!

Clinic Trainer

Horse clinics have become a thriving industry within the horse world. In order to conduct these educational sessions as a business, you need to prove yourself knowledgeable in a certain area, and it is best to get some qualifications. Your clinics may consist of hands-on work with people's horses or simply instructing people about their own horses. You should be organized, able to communicate and willing to publicize yourself and your clinics in order to fill them. Unless you have your own yard and plan to conduct all your clinics there – which limits your customer base dramatically – you need to travel around the country and find places to hire or sponsors for your clinics. It is a hard job, but it can be extremely rewarding to help people have safer and better experiences with horses.

Riding Instructor

If you have become an expert in a particular discipline, a career as a riding instructor may be just right for you. Good riders are always trying to better their skills. You don't have to have competed in the Olympics to help people be better riders (although you may get more publicity and more customers that way!).

You will need to have a place to offer classes, whether at your own yard or by hiring someone else's. Alternatively, you can get a job as a trainee instructor at a riding school and work your way up through the exams that way. Access to an indoor arena is useful in order to keep your business going through the winter. (You also need to be willing to stand out in the cold all day.)

The British Horse Society (*www.bhs.org.uk*) and the Association of British Riding Schools (*www.abrs.org.uk*) can provide you with more information on qualifying as an instructor.

Once you are qualified, your instruction programme can be set up in numerous ways. Many people work out how much time per week they can spend teaching riding and fill in the slots as customers come along. Generally, you will make more per hour with group lessons, although freelance instructors may also charge by the hour, and it is the riders who benefit from this – if there are several, each one pays less.

Horse Trainer

Perhaps you like working with young horses and would like to make a living at starting horses under saddle. This is perhaps one of the hardest – and one of the most rewarding – ways to make a living with horses. If you become very good, your services will be in great demand.

A so-called professional horse trainer (usually self-proclaimed, since there is no official certification required to set up as a horse trainer) trains other people's horses for a fee. The traditional scenario for years went like this: if you bought a young horse who had never been started under saddle, you sent him away to a horse trainer who specialized in the discipline you were interested in – for example, showing or dressage. Three months later, with perhaps a couple of visits in between, your trainer called you to tell you that your horse was ready and you could pick him up. You picked your horse up and rode off into the sunset, occasionally maybe sending him back to the trainer for a tune-up.

Like other equine professions in which you work directly with the horse, you will need an appropriate place to work with horses as a trainer, either by building and owning a place, or by renting one.

This scenario is no longer the only one. If you wish to be a horse trainer, you should be prepared for customers who want to be involved in their horse's training. They are not willing to just disappear for three months and not care what you are doing with their horse as long as the horse comes back rideable. Owners these days tend to not only care but also want to learn to work with their own horse and be able to understand the process of educating a horse to riding. This is where clinics come in, too.

Breeder

Involvement in horse breeding can be approached in two ways: you can be a veterinarian who specializes in reproduction, or you can learn a lot about genetics and breed, raise, and sell your own horses.

What does no fee for return stand for?

No fee for return means that if the mare doesn't become pregnant on the first visit to the stallion, the owner is allowed to bring her back until she does become pregnant. You will be expected to offer this facility if you have a stallion at stud.

Breeding and selling horses can be a complex undertaking. Generally, you choose a breed, maybe two, to specialize in. You will want to learn a lot about equine genetics in order to be able to choose the best pairings of stallions and mares.

To have a breeding programme, you will probably keep a stallion on the premises. Learn how to handle a stallion and perfect your handling abilities accordingly. You can also carry out your breeding programme with a complement of mares who get artificially inseminated.

Don't Stop Here

If nothing mentioned so far interests you, put on your thinking cap and see if you can come up with other ideas for making a living involving equines. You can be a researcher, an archaeologist researching horse history, a supplier of herbs for horses, a show judge – the list is only as limited as your imagination!

Resources

Magazines

The magazines listed below are all monthly, except *Horse and Hound*, which is weekly.

Eventing
Horse
Horse and Hound
Horse and Rider
Pony Magazine
You and Your Horse

Books and videos

There are literally hundreds of good books written about horses and/or riding; the titles below are just the tip of the iceberg. The best places to buy horse books are through a book club, via the British Horse Society bookshop (see address overleaf) or from Amazon (*www.amazon.co.uk*), where you might be able to find them available at a discount or secondhand. Unfortunately, the choice available in most high street bookshops is very limited. Some of the authors below have produced instructional videos. Again, the best way to find these is through the routes outlined above.

Bailey, Lesley, *The Photographic Guide to Schooling Your Horse*
Boone, J. Allen, *Kinship with All Life*
British Horse Society, *Riding and Roadcraft*
Bromiley, Mary, *Natural Methods for Equine Health*
Budiansky, Stephen, *The Nature of Horses*

Dorrance, Bill, and Desmond, Leslie, *True Horsemanship Through Feel*
Dorrance, Tom, *True Unity: Willing Communication Between Horse and Human*
Edwards, Elwyn Hartley, *Horses*
Edwards, Elwyn Hartley, *New Encyclopedia of the Horse*
Edwards, Elwyn Hartley, *The Horse Lover's Encylopedia*
Ganton, Doris, *Breaking and Training the Driving Horse*
Gray, Peter, *Essential Care of the Ridden Horse*
Griffin, James, and Gore, Tom, *Horse Owner's Veterinary Handbook*
Hempfling, Klaus Ferdinand, *Dancing with Horses*
Hunt, Ray, *Think Harmony with Horses: An In-depth Study of Horse/Man Relationship*
Jackson, Jamie, *The Natural Horse*
Kamen, Daniel, *The Well-Adjusted Horse*
McBane, Sue, and Davis, Caroline, *Complementary Therapies for Horse and Rider*
McCall, Jim, *Influencing Horse Behaviour*
Maltz, Maxwell, *Psycho-Cybernetics*
Marks, Kelly, *Perfect Manners*
Maxell, Richard, and Sharples, Johanna, *Unlock Your Horse's Talent in 20 Minutes a Day*
Moffett, Heather, *Enlightened Equitation*
Morrison, Liz, *Simple Steps to Riding Success*
Pavord, Marcy and Pavord, Tony, *Complete Equine Veterinary Manual*
Peace, Michael, and Bailey, Lesley, *Think Like Your Horse*

Podhajsky, Alois, *My Horses, My Teachers*
Rashid, Mark, *A Good Horse is Never a Bad Colour*
Rashid, Mark, *Considering Horses*
Rashid, Mark, *Horses Never Lie*
Rees, Lucy, *The Fundamentals of Riding*
Rees, Lucy, *The Horse's Mind*
Rees, Lucy, *Understanding Your Pony*
Roberts, Monty, *Join Up*
Roberts, Monty, *The Man Who Listens to Horses*
Savoie, Jane, *It's Not Just About the Ribbons*
Savoie, Jane, *That Winning Feeling: Program Your Mind for Peak Performance*
Swift, Sally, *Centred Riding* and *Centred Riding 2*
Swift, Sally, *Simplify Your Riding*
Tellington-Jones, Linda, *Getting in Touch with Horses*
Tellington-Jones, Linda, *Improve Your Horse's Wellbeing*
Tellington-Jones, Linda, *The Tellington Ttouch*
The Manual of Horsemanship (The Official Manual of the Pony Club)
Vogel, Colin, *RSPCA Complete Horse Care Manual*
Vogel, Colin, *The Horse's Health Bible*
Walrond, Sally, *A Guide to Driving Horses*
Wanless, Mary, *For the Good of the Horse*
Wanless, Mary, *For the Good of the Rider*
Wanless, Mary, *Ride with Your Mind*
Wood, Perry, *Real Riding: How to Ride in Harmony with Horses*

Useful Addresses and Websites

Associations and Societies
Association of British Riding Schools
Queen's Chambers
38/40 Queen Street
Penzance
Cornwall TR18 4BH
tel 01736 369440
www.abrs.org.uk

British Horse Society
Stoneleigh Park
Kenilworth
Warwickshire CV8 2XZ
tel 08701 202244
www.bhs.org.uk

British Dressage
National Agricultural Centre
Stoneleigh Park
Warwickshire CV8 2RJ
tel 024 7669 8830
www.britishdressage.co.uk
British Eventing
National Agricultural Centre
Stoneleigh Park
Warwickshire CV8 2RN
tel 024 7669 8856
www.britisheventing.co.uk

British Showjumping Association
National Agricultural Centre
Stoneleigh Park
Warwickshire CV8 2RJ
tel 024 7669 8800
www.bsja.co.uk

The Equestrian Society (Book Club)
Brunel House
Newton Abbot
Devon TQ12 1BR
tel 0870 4422123

Other
www.horseandhound.co.uk
www.horseit.com

Robinsons (mail-order horse equipment and clothing)
tel. 0870 420 3000
www.robinsons-uk.com

Glossary

Alternative medicine: Refers to diagnostic and treatment systems not commonly taught in medical/veterinary schools, such as nutrition, herbal medicine, homeopathy and chiropractic.

Amino acids: The group of organic compounds that form the structure of proteins. Alfalfa and clover are rich in amino acids and gives horses extra energy.

Azoturia: Also known as 'tying up' or 'Monday morning disease', azoturia refers to the cramping of a horse's large hindquarter muscles.

Blacksmith: A blacksmith is not a horseshoer but someone who makes things with iron.

Breeding stock: A mare or stallion that is intended for breeding work. Breeding stock are usually selected for their good conformation or other qualities that will make their offspring attractive to prospective purchasers.

Choke: A condition that is often caused when horses gulp down hard feeds too rapidly. To deter this, place a couple of stones in the feed bucket – having to eat around them makes the horse slow down.

Conditioned response: A training approach in which a horse (or any thinking animal, including humans) is conditioned to respond to the same stimulus the same way every time she confronts that stimulus.

Conformation: The overall structure of the horse is known as its conformation. Few horses, if any, have perfect conformation. What is considered good conformation depends a great deal on what you plan to do with the horse.

Farrier: A farrier is a blacksmith who does horseshoeing but doesn't necessarily do other types of iron work.

Flehman response: A term that refers to the curling of the upper lip by a male horse in response to the scent of a female.

Groundwork: The practice of teaching your horse at the end of a lead rope. Many of the things you teach him in groundwork are transferable to the saddle.

Hand: In tack room terms, a hand is the unit used to measure horse height. One hand equals 10cm (4in); thus, a horse that stands 15 hands tall is 1.5m (5ft).

Herbivore: An animal that subsists totally on plant life. Horses are herbivores. This distinction makes the horse a prey animal, a fact that contributes greatly to the overall behaviour of the species.

Hogging: Hogging refers to a mane that has been completely shaved.

Proud flesh: A wound that won't heal produces scar tissue that protrudes from the wound area. This scar tissue is commonly referred to as 'proud flesh'.

Psychocybernetics: The technique for using your subconscious power to achieve the positive results that you desire.

Rails: The individual horizontal bars that make up a jump. They can easily be removed or added to make the jump lower or higher.

Sound: If the horse is perfectly healthy, it is said to be sound.

Tree: The basic structure, usually made of wood or fibreglass, that saddles are built upon. They can be narrow or wide, depending on the type of horse and the comfort of the rider.

Turnout: The period when your horse is out of the confinement of her stable and loose in a larger area – either outside in a paddock or perhaps in an indoor arena if the weather is bad.

Unsound: If the horse is temporarily lame or has some other health problems , it is considered unsound. Anything that adversely affects a horse's health is considered an unsoundness. If the horse's problem is chronic, the horse is permanently unsound.

Index